CW01471655

Layman's Guide to Irish Law

The Law of Tort

Teresa Clyne BA, MSc

These books are written "as is", they are compiled for a novice, in basic introductory or note form with a breakdown of each subject, the language is casual and conversational, similar to how you would chat to your friends over lunch on the subject, with some truncated sentences, bullet style explanations and paragraphs, there are truncated case synopsis with occasional ellipses. Headers include examples and explanations with real life scenarios; for that reason, these books are not academic textbooks, merely informational.

"To all who dream in part, in the hope that they may attain someone else's experience in the delights and dangers of an adventure, also to my amazing kids and grandkids for without whose endless empathy, sympathy and encouragement this book would have been finished in half the time". ~

Nostrae Theresiae

Laws are partly formed for the sake of good men, in order to instruct them how they may live on friendly terms with one another, and partly for the sake of those who refuse to be instructed, whose spirit cannot be subdued, or softened, or hindered from plunging into evil. ~

Plato

Disclaimer:

No liability is accepted by Teresa Clyne BA, MSc for any action taken or not taken in reliance on the information set out in this publication. Any and all information is subject to change and professional or legal advice should be obtained before taking or refraining from any action as a result of the contents of this publication. This book is written in spoken English and is intended to help lay (non-legal) persons who want to understand the very basics of the law of tort

This is not an academic textbook; it is a very basic foot in the door of contract law and the authorities that deal with it, however, some beginners may find it helps them in the early stages of their studies or those taking introductory courses in law or accounting

Printed in the Republic of Ireland

Introduction

Foreword

This Introduction to Irish law book is a handy little number, it is compiled so that the most difficult and challenging terminology, rules and principles are explained, leaving you to enjoy learning about the law in Ireland without the headache of first learning terminology and confounding principles.

Torts are wrongdoings; done by one person against another. When one person wrongs another, the injured person may take civil action against the other person. In plain English, let's say while walking down the fruit and veg aisle of your local supermarket, you slip on a grape that had fallen from the shelf and injure yourself. You become the **plaintiff**, or injured party, and the supermarket is considered the **tortfeasor** or **defendant**, they are defined as the negligent party. When this happens you can take civil action against the supermarket to claim compensation for pain, suffering, medical bills and expenses incurred as a result of the fall. Negligence is just one tort category. This book will go through all of the different types.

The Law of Tort

Torts are concerned with civil wrongs, whereby one-party causes damage to another party.

- Tort is the French word for a "wrong" or Latin for "twisted".
- Tort is a branch of Civil Law; therefore, a tort in law is called a "Civil Wrong"
- Tort law protects a variety of injuries and provides remedies (*ways to fix*) them.

Torts can be distinguished from legal wrongs:

A Tort is **not** a **breach of contract**, where the obligation which is alleged to have been breached arose under an agreement between two parties.

A Tort is **not** a **crime**, where the object of proceedings is to punish the offender rather than compensate the victim.

Using tort law, an injured party can bring a civil case to seek compensation for a wrong done to the party (*plaintiff, or injured party*) or the party's property. Tort damages or compensation are monetary damages that are sought from the offending party. They are intended to compensate the injured party for the injury suffered.

Intentional torts; such as trespass, nuisance, false imprisonment, passing off, defamation,

Unintentional torts, such as negligence,

Strict liability torts, for example: manufacturer's product liability.

Example: *To simplify this, let's say while you were shopping in your local supermarket, you slip on a banana that had fallen from a shelf. You become the plaintiff, or injured party, and the supermarket is considered the tortfeasor or defendant, "the negligent party". Basically, you would probably take civil action (personal injury claim) against the supermarket to seek compensation for pain, suffering, medical bills and expenses incurred as a result of the fall.*

The Law of Tort

What is the law of tort all about?

Tort deals with claims by private persons against other parties (*individuals, organisations, etc...*)

- The main objective is compensation not punishment
- There are some equitable (*fair and just*) remedies available (*injunctions etc.*)
- It has a long history – mostly case law
- There is some recent legislation (*occupiers' liability and liability for defective products*)
- There is an importance of "*fault principle*"
- Negligence accounts for most claims
- It is classed as corrective justice which rights wrongs

Negligence is just one tort category. There are three general categories of torts. Regardless of the tort action, three elements must be present: (see above supermarket example)

- Tortfeasor, or defendant, (*supermarket*) had a duty to act or behave in a certain way. (*take care when going about their business*)
- Plaintiff (the injured party) must prove that the behaviour taken by the tortfeasor, or a defendant (supermarket) did not conform to the duty owed to the plaintiff. (*they did not act in the way a reasonable supermarket would*)
- The plaintiff (*injured party*) suffered an injury or loss as a result (*because the supermarket acted in a negligent manner, "not cleaning up the banana").*

Because torts are civil actions involving private parties (*individuals*), retribution (*punishment*) does not include a criminal fine or a prison sentence. The punishment for tortious acts usually involves restoring the injured party monetarily (*financially*). Sometimes a court order may force the tortfeasor (*defendant or negligent party*) to either do or not do something by issuing (*injunctions called mandatory "you must do something" and prohibitory "you must NOT do something*"). For instance; you must not trespass, defame or slander another person.

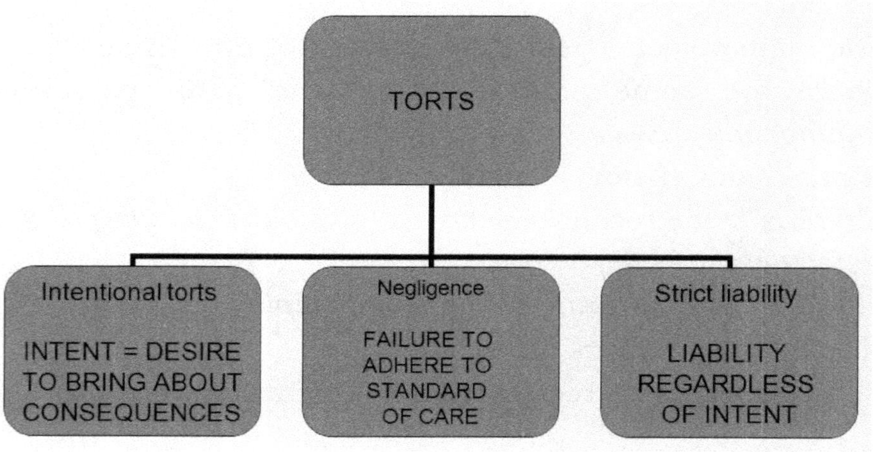

Firstly, we will deal with the three types of torts:

1. Intentional torts *(When the defendant causes an injury on purpose, for example, hitting someone or saying things about them that are not true).*

2. Unintentional torts *(Unintentional torts are accidents; they happen because someone was not being careful. When a person is not being careful, it is called acting **negligently**).*

3. Strict liability torts *(Strict liability does not require any proof or intention to commit a wrong or act negligently)*

Aims of Tort

Compensation - to compensate the victim of the wrong to the extent of the damage suffered!

Deterrence / prevention – this is to ensure that it does not happen again or, even better, to prevent it from occurring at all.

The Law of Tort

How does a tort differ from a crime?

A tort will lead the wronged party to try and recover money as compensation for the loss or injury suffered.

A tort does not, however, call upon the state to punish the wrongdoer.

Types of Tort

Intentional Torts

An intentional tort occurs when one person (*the defendant, the wrongdoer*) intentionally commits a tort (*wrong*) against another person (*plaintiff, or injured party*) with the ***intention*** of causing harm.

There are many intentional torts such as, assault, battery, conversion, fraud, false imprisonment, trespassing, defamation and invasion of privacy. In order for a claim to fall into intentional torts the intention of the defendant (*wrongdoer)* will be looked at by the court to determine if the defendant intended to do the harm or if they were just being reckless *(negligent)*.

Trespass is an area of tort law broadly divided into three groups:

Trespass to a person, assault, battery, false imprisonment.

- Trespass to the person,
- Trespass to chattels and
- Trespass to land.

Defamation –Libel and Slander are now one tort of defamation

Unintentional Torts

Unintentional torts of referred to as negligence. These are accidents, where the wrongdoer (*defendant*) did not intend for the damage or wrong to happen.

Negligence *is as a result of conduct that falls below the standard of care which is demanded for the protection of others against the unreasonable risk of harm. The test in negligence;*

...the plaintiff (persons suffering from the harm) must show that the defendant (person causing the harm) owed them a duty of care; and.
...they breached that duty of care, (by falling below the standard of care); and;
...their breach caused the other person injuries; and;
...caused them to suffer reasonably foreseeable harm (damage was not too remote).

Unintentional torts include car accidents and slips and falls, this happens when the defendant has not taken the care required to ensure that other persons do not get hurt.

When determining if a defendant has acted negligently the court will examine if the defendant acted the way a ***reasonable person*** would have under those circumstances, or not acted in those particular circumstances.

Strict Liability Torts

Strict liability holds a person responsible for the damages or loss caused by his or her acts (*something they did*) or omissions (*something they failed to do*). This doctrine (*principle or rule*) holds a person liable irrespective of fault (*whether they actually did anything to cause the damage*). Strict liability in tort law is important in product liability (*liability for defective products*). Strict liability in tort is the doctrine (*rule*) that imposes liability on a party or a person (*defendant*) without the court having to examine the case and find fault. If the court examines the case and finds fault, then the case is no longer strict liability and reverts to negligence or intent. In strict liability cases the wronged person (*plaintiff*) only needs to prove only that the tort happened, and that the defendant was responsible.

Strict liability occurs where a manufacturer is liable for the products they make, if anything happens to a person using them the court does not need to prove any fault, the manufacturer made it, and the consumer bought it, and the customer was injured while using it in a reasonably foreseeable way—even if the product was not being used for its intended purpose, no other fault is required, (*the manufacturer is not required to have intended that a person would get injured.*) Where a dog bites a person, no matter how well trained the dog is or how many precautions the owner took in controlling them, if the dog bites anyone, then the owner is liable, again, no fault is required, the fact is the owner had a dog, the dog bit another person, this is called strict liability in tort. Strict liability deters reckless behaviour and encourages parties to take extra care to prevent damage or injury.

Trespass to the Person

Intentional Torts

Trespass to the person

The acts of **battery**, **assault** and **false imprisonment** are commonly considered within the scope of trespass to the person. You should note that the acts may also result in a criminal action against the defendant. *Devlin v Roche [2002]*[1] stated that assault/battery is distinct from negligence.

1. **Battery**

Battery involves the **intentional** bringing of a material object into contact with another person. **Battery** occurs when one person unlawfully touches another person. It is intentional and direct application of force (*bringing an actual item in contact with the body of another person*)

Elements of battery are:

- The mental state of the defendant
- The defendant's act was under his control
- Contact
- Without plaintiff's consent/permission

2. **Assault**

Assault is the intentional act of putting another in **reasonable fear or apprehension of immediate battery**. Words may not be enough to create a liability unless they are accompanied by menacing or threatening actions. For example, telling someone you will shoot them may not be classed as assault unless you are pointing a gun at them as well. [2]Assault is an act, which causes another person to apprehend the infliction of immediate[3], unlawful force ***(Collins v Wilcock [1984])***[4]**.**

---

[1] *Devlin v Roche [2002] 2 IR 367*
[2] *http://www.margarethagan.com/*
[3] *Emphasis is on **immediate** battery*
[4] *Collins v Wilcock [1984]1 WLR 1172*

Thomas v National Union of Mine Workers [1985] [5] *(would a reasonable person apprehend immediate battery?)*

[5] *Thomas v National Union of Mine Workers [1985] 2 All ER 1*

S 2(1) of the Non-Fatal Offences Against the Person Act 2007.

2.—(1) A person shall be guilty of the offence of assault who, without lawful excuse, intentionally (*meaning to*) or recklessly (*not considering how their actions or omission would affect others*)—directly or indirectly applies force to or causes an impact on the body of another, or causes another to believe on reasonable grounds that he or she is likely immediately to be subjected to any such force or impact, without the consent of the other. A case of intentional tort of trespass is where a person intentionally, and without the consent of the other person, applies direct force to the body of another.

3. **False imprisonment**

False Imprisonment – to restrict a person's movement (arresting, imprisoning or preventing person from leaving)

Elements in False Imprisonment are:

- *Intention is essential*
- *The restraint must be a direct result of the defendant's act*

The restraint must be complete

False imprisonment involves **unlawfully arresting**, **imprisoning** or **preventing a person from leaving** from where they are. The plaintiff does not have to prove damage was caused as it was their liberty that was taken from them.

Trespass to the person is a tort of intention, there must be an intention to harm, (*even if no actual physical harm occurs*), traditionally this tort involved six separate trespasses: threats, assault (*fear of, or imminent battery*), battery (*physical harm, i.e. punch or sexual assault*), **Stubbings v Webb [1993]**[6]. (*The court stated that sexual abuse and rape perpetrated by an adoptive father and stepbrother fell within trespass*) wounding, mayhem (*chaos*), and maiming (*disfigurement*).

Self-defence, (*no consent is required*), is a valid defence to trespasses to the person, supposing the party used "reasonable force which they honestly and reasonably believe is necessary to protect themselves or

[6] *Stubbings v Webb [1993] AC 498*

someone else, or property". (*The force used must be equal to the threat*). Unlawful detention (*custody*) or restraint of liberty (*freedom*) of a person.[7]

- restraint must be total
- the only means of escape is unreasonable
- person who continues the imprisonment commits the tort
- may be physical or psychological
- generally, it is not false imprisonment to fail to release someone on personal property, ***Burns v Johnston***[8]

[7] *Unlawful and **total** restraint of the personal liberty of another*
[8] *Burns v Johnston [1917] 2 IR 137*

Threats

Threats are not generally classed as assault unless it can be proven that those words would make a reasonable person apprehend an ***immediate*** battery[9]. *i.e. lads get the guns out.*

Silent phone calls

Silent phone calls can be defined as assault due to the apprehension a person may feel, the apprehension must make them apprehend that they are in ***immediate*** danger of battery. ***R v Ireland [1998]*** [10]

Trespass torts in medicine

Negligence and the issue of consent

- A doctor that administers any form of treatment that results in contact with plaintiff's person can be liable for battery
- Cause of action: trespass or negligence? ***Walsh v Family Planning Services (Orr and Kelly)***[11] (*plaintiff's claim in trespass and negligence, failing to advise patients of the risks of treatment, appropriate cause is negligence, not trespass, Supreme Court limited doctor's liability in trespass*)

---

[9] *Emphasis is on immediate battery*

[10] *R v Ireland [1998] AC 147 fear of immediate personal violence.*

[11] *Walsh v Family Planning Service [1992] 1 IR 496, Walsh claimed trespass where a vasectomy went wrong, as he was not warned if this particular danger, which was very rare, court held: it was negligence, not trespass.*

Defences to the tort of trespass

Consent

- main defence to trespass claim
- medical context: must be voluntary, interventions on the consent of adults (*over 16 medically*) can be allowed if they are in the best interests of the person
- capacity of minors: minor must be able to understand what the procedure involves giving consent, parent/guardian can give consent, court can overrule decision against life-saving treatment, ***Gillick v West Norfolk and Wisbech Area Health Authority*** (*competent minors can give consent if they are under the age of 16 if they understand the nature of the treatment*), no direct Irish authority (apply Gillick), best interests and constitutional elements.
- Medical treatment may not be given to an adult person of full capacity without his or her consent. ***RE: A Ward of Court (withholding medical treatment) (No.2) [1996]***[12]

Defences to tort of trespass

a) Consent (agreed to it)
b) Self-defence (had to protect themselves)
c) Defence of third parties (had to do it to protect another person)
d) Lawful arrest (citizen's arrest, only when they believe they have, or are about to, commit a criminal offence)
e) Defence of property (stop someone from damaging their property)
f) Duress (under pressure, threatened if they did not commit the tort)

Self-defence

Fawcitt J in ***Dullaghan v Hillen*** (*self-defence definition: when wrongfully assaulted it is lawful to repel force provided no unnecessary violence is used.)* How much force, what kind is used and whether it is reasonable depend on the circumstances and fact. Force used in defence must be equal to the force which provoked it.

---

[12] *RE: A Ward of Court (withholding medical treatment) (No.2) [1996] 2 IR 79*

(**For example:** *the old saying, don't bring a gun to a knife fight. You are required to fight like with like or a reasonable alternative.)*

Defence of Third Persons

The same reasoning as self-defence

- Necessity
- Scope is uncertain
- Beyond clear medical case unlikely to be recognised as a defence

Rigby v Chief Constable (*police accidentally set a shop on fire to flush out a psychopath, the court held that they were not liable in trespass, relying on necessity, but were liable in negligence, as they had failed to provide sufficient fire-fighting equipment*).

Lawful Authority

Not usually liable, e.g., the Gardaí

Defence of Property

- If a person enters forcibly into the land belonging to someone else, the other person may use reasonable force to get the person off their land (*reasonable force depends on the circumstances*)

- If a person enters without force but does not leave when requested, the other person may use reasonable force to get the person to leave (*reasonable force dependant on circumstances*) ***MacKnight v Xtravision***

Defences to the Tort of Trespass

Duress (pressure or threat)

- When a person harms another person while under duress the courts will balance between competing interests, i.e. was the pressure or threat sufficient to deem the harm a defence.

Trespass to Land

Trespass to land, this form of trespass is most associated with the term 'trespass', it refers to the "wrongful interference with one's possessory rights in [real] property. The Irish constitution states that we have the right to private property without intrusion.

For example: *Hillwalkers must understand that trespassing on private farmland is an intrusion (disturbance), an intrusion on farmers' rights and livelihoods (earning a living). For instance, hill walkers going through fields and leaving gates open not only disturb farmers but could allow livestock to escape and cause damage or be killed or even that other animals could get onto the land and cause damage.* Trespass to land involves **one** or a **combination** of the following acts without lawful justification:

1. **Entering** land that is owned by the plaintiff.
2. **Remaining** on the land.
3. **Placing** objects or projections onto the land

There are several defences to trespass to land; license, justification by law, the necessity and ***jus tertii***. (Latin, "third party rights") ***License*** is express (spoken or written) or implied (*unspoken or unwritten, inferred from the action or understood through use and time*) permission, given by the possessor of land, to be on that land. These licenses are irrevocable (*cannot be taken back or changed*) unless there is a flaw (*error or mistake*) in the agreement or it is given by a contract (*signed document*). Once revoked (*taken back or withdrawn*), a license-holder becomes a trespasser if they remain on the land.

If someone entering onto the premises is not there by as of right or invitation (*a visitor*) nor are they there as a recreational user (i.e. to look at an area of natural beauty) then they are a trespasser in civil law under the occupiers liability act, 1995. This can be seen clearly in cases such as ***Williams v. TP Wallace Construction & Others.***

This contrasts (*compares the rights of*) with the landowner who has the power to control and an occupier who is *'a person exercising such control over the state of the premises that is it reasonable to impose upon that person a duty towards an entrant, whether the entrant concerned is a visitor, recreational user or trespasser.'*

"**recreational activity**" means any recreational activity conducted, whether alone or with others, in the open air (including any sporting activity), scientific research and nature study so conducted, exploring caves and visiting sites and buildings of historical, architectural, traditional, artistic, archaeological or scientific importance;

"**recreational user**" means an entrant who, with or without the occupier's permission or at the occupier's implied invitation, is present on premises without a charge (other than a reasonable charge in respect of the cost of providing vehicle parking facilities) being imposed for the purpose of engaging in a recreational activity, including an entrant admitted without charge to a national monument pursuant to section 16 (1) of ***the National Monuments Act, 1930*** , but not including an entrant who is so present and is—

- a member of the occupier's family who is ordinarily resident on the premises,
- an entrant who is present at the express invitation of the occupier or such a member, or
- an entrant who is present with the permission of the occupier or such a member for social reasons connected with the occupier or such a member;

Trespass is a criminal offence if it is done to cause fear in another person or in circumstances which give rise to a reasonable inference[13] (*conclusion of a reasonable person*) that they were there to commit an offence under ***the Public Order Act, 1994***.

[13] Reasonable inferences mean "conclusions which are regarded as logical by reasonable people in the light of their experience in life." [Lannon v. Hogan, 719 F.2d 518, 521 (1st Cir. Mass. 1983)]

Trespass to Land

Entering a premises without lawful authority intending to commit a serious offence or while there actually committing a serious offence is ***burglary***.

Trespass to Goods

Trespass to chattels (*personal goods, they can be touched and seen, i.e. a car, a watch, a vase*), also known as trespass to goods or trespass to personal property. Trespass to chattels, does not require a showing of damages. Simply, the "intermeddling (*interfere with someone else's property*) with or use of the personal property" of another allows the chattel owner the right to bring a case against the wrongdoer. Trespass to goods means; *'Direct, immediate interference with personal property belonging to another person'.*

It must also be identified as ownership and not merely possession. A person can have possession of an item, say another person's coat, however they may not own it and therefore have no legal right to keep it. Therefore, this distinction is vital, there is a difference between a right of ownership and a right of enjoyment.

This tort allows the owner to get their property back immediately, it resembles trespass to land.

Conversion

Conversion

Conversion is one person taking someone else's property and using it for their own personal gain. It is dealing with the personal goods of another person denying the right of the owner to the goods. Only the owner of the goods can bring a claim for conversion. **For Example**: *if a farmer has 9 large trees growing on their property, another neighbour cuts them down, the neighbour may be liable for conversion, even if they don't use the trees, they denied the owner use of the trees even if it was only for shade or producing fruit.*

However, in limited circumstances a person who is entitled to the goods who has not yet got possession of them can also bring a claim. **For example**: *If I had agreed to sell you my lawnmower and you were on your way to pick it up and pay me, my neighbour pops in and takes it to his house and when you get there, it's not in the shed, you find out the neighbour has it, you are entitled to go and take it back as you were entitled to possession after payment.*

The owner must prove that he had possession of the goods or the right to immediate possession of them at the time of the other person took the goods and used for their own gain.

Sample conversion

- Contradicting the title of the true owner
- Detaining goods belonging to the owner without permission after a demand for the goods which has been refused.
- Destruction of goods belonging to the owner
- Selling goods without the owner's permission.

Remedy for conversion *(a right is enforced, or an injury is redressed)*

Damages obtainable for conversion based on the recovery of the market value of the goods and special damages, the true owner of the goods can have them given back plus special damages.

Conversion

- An order for delivery of the goods in the course of an interim (*temporary*) application
- An order plus damages (compensation) or with damages as an alternative.

Chose in action

Chose in Action (*Intangible Property - Transferable by assignment*)

A chose in action is a legal right to sue for intangible rights (things which you cannot touch or see but nonetheless exist), such things as copyright, IP rights, patents, intellectual property as well as debts and shares, electricity, also, insurance policies, confidential information and computer programs are also intangible assets. When a person brings a chose in action and is successful the ownership of the intangible property is assigned to them, as no physical presence in present.

Choses in action can only be enforced by an action, this means a person cannot gain physical right to the property, and they can however use a chose in action to have the intangible property converted to physical money and gain possession.

A share can also be intangible, as can stocks; (once they are transferable.i.e. the ownership can be transferred to another person), however a savings bond cannot as it is *non-transferable*. These rights can only be enforced by action (bringing a legal case) and no actual physical possession is taken.

These rights can be legal or equitable. These rights include rights to:

- Shares
- Money due (debt)
- Rights/benefits under a contract
- Mortgagor's equity of redemption
- Beneficiary's rights and interests under a trust

Trespass to goods

Trespass to Goods – Detinue

Wrongful failure/refusal, to return goods when demand a has been made for same. The plaintiff must be in possession or have an immediate claim for possession.

A reasonable period of time for return is allowed. Each case is taken on its own merit, i.e. reasonable time for fast moving consumer goods will not be the same as for furniture, and the reasonable time is relative to the case.

The tests for detinue are:

- Possession
- Demand made
- Demand received
- Refusal or failure to return
- No excuse of necessity, authority etc.

Defences to Private Nuisance

Nuisance

The tort of nuisance is easily distinguishable from trespass insofar as, interference which gives rise to nuisance is typically indirect; unlike trespass which is direct.

Also, nuisance can be distinguished from negligence due to the intention which is usually present in nuisance.

Finally, it may be distinguished from the rule in **Rylands v. Fletcher**[14] in that in nuisance accumulation of harmful things or substances is not required; similarly escape of the accumulated thing is not required, though in many instances escape of accumulated things also occurs. However, it must be noted cases which present the same set of facts may give rise to liability under nuisance, and under ***Rylands v. Fletcher and Connolly v South of Ireland Asphalt Co:***

Nuisance is an act or omission which amounts to an unreasonable interference with, disturbance *of*, or annoyance *to* another person in the exercise of their rights associated with enjoyment of their property.

Private Nuisance

A private nuisance is a continuous, *unlawful and indirect interference with the use or enjoyment of land*, or of some right over or in connection with it.

Private nuisance is actionable only as a tort. It involves rights relating to ownership, occupation or personal interests in connection with land. Though initially concerned with protecting people from interference in relationship to ownership of land, private nuisance now extends to enjoyment of personal interests connected with the land.

---

*The **Rylands v. Fletcher [1868]** case introduced into law a specific type of nuisance, one which is strict liability, the defendant may be liable even in the absence of any negligence on the defendant's part. This imposition of liability has caused this case to be what can only amount of one of the most controversial and most used cases in the history of the study of Negligence and Tort.*

Defences to Private Nuisance

The following factors must be considered in a nuisance action:

1. Locus Standi;
2. Conduct - acts or omissions;
3. Damage or Interference;
4. Strict liability for Material Damage;
5. Liability for interference with enjoyment judged by standard of unreasonable impact.

Locus Standi

Legal standing (it must be the plaintiff's case, or they are entitled to bring the case). In Ireland, as in England, exclusive possession of the land must be shown to ground a nuisance action. ***Hanrahan v. Merck Sharpe and Dohme (1988)*** established that a plaintiff in Ireland merely needs to show occupation of premises

Omissions

Harrington v. Cork County Council (2005) Liability can also include the failure to alleviate natural hazards, omissions to alleviate risks caused by third parties, failure to repair the property, or failure to act on a disruptive state of affairs. Caravans were present on land adjoining to a business, which then sued the defendant, the court found for the plaintiff, holding that the council had not taken all reasonable steps to alleviate the nuisance; the court granted an injunction requiring the defendant to take all reasonable steps to remove the trespassers and to prevent further occurrences, as well as abating the nuisance by cleaning up the area. In the case of multiple offenders, for instance, plaintiff and defendant, the party actively creating the nuisance is most likely to be held liable.

For example: *If you have large trees which are overhanging the public road and they are becoming old and dangerous, you are obliged to ensure that those trees do not fall onto the public road and hurt anyone,* *also if they were low hanging and people had to walk onto the highway off the path to avoid them you have not attempted to alleviate the risk which you are obliged to do.*

Damage or Interference

The plaintiff must prove damage to recover damages or to have an injunction granted. In historical cases, damage was presumed based on geography and the circumstances, in the same vein as ***res ipsa***. However, this need not be proved in the case of a right of way claim.

The types of damages are as follows:

Material Damage

This is damage to the actual land, and to property including chattels, e.g. **For example:** *a claimant was able to recover for damage done to their cattle and land caused by toxic emissions from a neighbouring factory.*

Defences to Private Nuisance

Interference with enjoyment

Halpin v. Tara Mines (1976); this extends to residents, occupiers, and also the dependents of the plaintiff. It is based on the "sensible discomfort to the reasonable man".

In The court examines the following factors in assessing whether the impact is reasonable:

1. Magnitude of harm;
2. Nature of locality;
3. Defendant's motives;
4. Social utility deciding if nuisance has occurred the courts will consider the following:

Magnitude of harm

The court will consider the intensity, duration and frequency of the interference at an objective standard. That is the standard of a reasonable person in the circumstances.

Nature of locality

The court will consider the general nature of the surroundings. Therefore, in ***O'Kane v. Campell (1985)***, despite the fact that the resident's lives near a busy thoroughfare, the court held this was not enough to diminish the fact that it was a residential neighbourhood.

Defendant's motives

The court will consider the defendant's motives (*the reason they did it*) in whether to award the damages (*money*) and injunctions (*make a person do something or stop them doing something*), for instances in the case of ***Sheeran v. Meehan (2003)*** the High Court allowed an injunction against the defendant, notwithstanding that he kept the noise to regulation levels, the injunction was granted as he kept the music levels "just below" the required levels and despite consistent requests did not turn it down any lower.

Social utility

Bellew v. Cement Ltd (1948): The courts will consider the social utility of the actions of the defendant before deciding if a remedy will be given, an injunction against noisy quarry works refused based on the urgent need for cement in the surrounding areas. **For example**: *the court will determine if the actions or inactions are in the best interest of the society as a whole.*

Defences to Private Nuisance

Consent

Where the claimant by their actions, consent to the nuisance, i.e. *Thomas v Lewis*: The defendant opened quarry & granted grazing rights to the claimant. **HELD:** When the claimant acceptance the grazing rights the consented to the acquiescence to the nuisance.

Prescription

If the nuisance has been continued for 20 years without interruption the defendant will not liable if s/he pleads a prescriptive right to the nuisance.

Statutory Authority

There will be a defence to private nuisance if it can be shown that the activities complained of by the claimant were authorised (expressly or impliedly) by a statute.

Coming to the nuisance is no defence.

The claimant moving to the area where the nuisance is occurring, is no defence. See above *Bliss v Hall*

Remedies for Private Nuisance

Remedies

Damages

Compensation –

The compensation will depend on the amount of damage done, i.e. interference with enjoyment will be amenity value (the value you placed on aesthetics, visual or quality of life)

Injunctions

Injunctions are equitable remedies given at the discretion of the court (*see law of equity in my Introduction to the Irish Legal System book*). They are **Mandatory** (*make you do something*) or **Prohibitory** (*stop you from doing something*). The difference between a mandatory and prohibitory: (*i.e. The council can get a mandatory injunction to make you clean your yard, whereas they cannot get a prohibitory injunction to stop you not cleaning your yard...!! And vice versa, the council can get a prohibitory injunction to stop you having farm animals at your urban house, whereas they cannot get a mandatory injunction to make you not have them...*)Due to the on-going nature of the tort, injunctions are often sought. This is an equitable remedy, and therefore a discretionary remedy, and may or may not be awarded in addition to damages.

Interim, these are emergency orders which are ordered to stop some act or omission immediately, there will then be an application for a:

Permanent injunction: an injunction which remains in force perpetually (*forever).*

Abatement

This is the remedy of self-help, e.g. removing over-hanging tree branches, which are a nuisance. (Make sure to return the branches to the owner)

Public Nuisance:

Public nuisance is defined as a criminal offence and also a tortious one. It involves and affects the rights of members of the general public or sections of the general public (or a considerable class thereof), the effects of public nuisance need not be in a particular geographical or social class, and nuisance can be indiscriminate and widespread in its effects.

A nuisance can become a public nuisance whether the effects on the public are from its source, its destination or the final effect. All public nuisance cases are looked at from the point of "reasonableness". Examples of public nuisance include, obstruction of public roads, obstruction of access to business access to workplaces, noises pollution, the enjoyment of paths, roads, parks, forests, it water supply contamination, oil spillage from the activities of large oil companies and this includes but is not limited to carrying on abhorrent business like operating a brothel. The Attorney General instigates public nuisance cases; however, members of the public may take cases, but must show he has suffered some *"special"* or *"particular"* damage, such as the recent cases brought by the residents of Croke Park for nuisance arising out of crowds and traffic congestion.

Cunningham v McGrath Brothers [1964]: The plaintiff left a ladder in the street which fell over and hurt a passer-by. **HELD:** The Court held in this case that any obstruction of a public highway is a nuisance. This tort comes into being when the defendant or any person acting on his behalf actively conducts the behaviour. There is no requirement to prove any negligence, the plaintiff merely needs to prove the defendant caused the plaintiff to lose the enjoyment of their land/property.

Recovery for

a) Personal injury, and

b) Damage to property, are frequently successful in cases of negligence.

Pure Economic Loss

The final note on nuisance is the court's stance on claims for pure economic loss, the decision in ***Tate v. Greater London Council (1983),*** confirmed that indeed it is possible to claim for pure economic loss, this case was brought by a business owner who had lost customers due to the obstruction of the highway by Greater London Council which resulted in him losing customers. **HELD:** the courts will impose liability for pure economic loss.

For example: *If a person is negligent and you suffer a financial loss and no physical damage whatsoever, then the courts will allow that you can claim for this.*

Remedies for Public Nuisance

Remedies

Damages

An award for damages can be sought by the plaintiff, however, these are minimal, they serve not to punish the wrong doer, but to encourage the defendant to take steps to negate or stop the nuisance.

Injunctions

Due to the on-going nature of the tort, injunctions are often sought. This is an equitable remedy, and therefore a discretionary remedy, and may or may not be awarded in addition to damages.

Interim, these are emergency orders which are ordered to stop some act or omission immediately, there will then be an application for a:

Permanent injunction; this is an injunction which remains in force perpetually.

Injunctions can consist of a;

Mandatory injunction, an order to compel the defendant to carry out a particular act, i.e. clear a pathway or roadway or a;

Prohibitory injunction, this injunction is ordered by the court to stop the defendant for committing an act, which occasionally can include noise abatement orders.

Nuisance – Private Tenants

Private Rented Tenants:

Those in private rented accommodation are dealt with by ***the Residential Tenancies Act 2004***. The act helps impose minimum obligations on landlords and tenants of private residential properties, i.e.: Tenants are not to engage, or allow visitors to engage, in anti-social behaviour, which disturbs the peace.

Landlords must enforce these tenant obligations:

There is also leverage in the act for people to complain to the Private Residential Tenancies Board, if they feel the landlord is not acting accordingly. Since December 2004, all privately-rented properties must be registered with the PRTB. The affected person can check if a property is registered by contacting them.

Local Authority Tenants:

Local authority tenants usually have regulations on their behaviour written into their tenancy agreement. This is the legal basis of the relationship between the local authority and its tenants. Local authorities' power, in this case, comes under ***Section 62 of the Housing Act 1966***. They have the authority to secure an eviction, where a tenant has breached the conditions of their tenancy agreement. The first point of contact, if the affected person has a complaint regarding a local authority tenant, is their local authority.

Private Homeowner:

Nuisance noise caused by a private homeowner comes under other regulations. In this case, the person experiencing the noise nuisance will have to avail of the powers of Noise Regulations. They state that any individual person, or a local authority, may complain to a District Court and seek an order to deal with the noise nuisance.

Alarms

For faulty alarms on commercial premises the local authority should be notified. If the alarm is on private property, the occupiers should be notified and only then if the problem persists can it be treated as a neighbourhood noise problem. Some local authorities have issued guidelines that owners/occupiers of alarmed property should nominate at least two key-holders who can be contacted in the event of the activation of the alarm. Local authorities may also serve a notice under the ***Environmental Protection Agency Act, 1992***. New, tougher measures were proposed by the previous Government, such as giving power to the Gardaí to turn off alarms - on the outside of premises - which are causing annoyance. No standards have been set for the operation of car alarms.

Passing Off – (copyright/patent theft or using a brand name to sell products)

(*The Tort of Deceit*) "Passing off" is a common law tort which can be used to enforce unregistered trademark rights, "Passing off" is a means whereby a seller induces another person to buy a product by misrepresenting that that product belongs to another. (i.e. backwards Nike symbol of clothing may induce a buyer to believe it is Nike because of their good name "Nike" or reputation they decide to buy it), it was a precursor to Copyright and Patent laws now in use. Also, products can be deemed to be misleading as in the case of *Campomar v Nike*[15], Campomar produced a fragrance under their brand Nike Sports Fragrances, it was sold in the same isle as other Nike products, the court held that the fragrance in the same isle as other Nike products would induce a reasonable person to believe that the fragrance was produced by Nike. "Passing off" is a misrepresentation made by one party which damages the goodwill of another party. This is done by one party passing off the other party's goods or services as their own.

Elements of Passing off

Traders are forbidden from selling their goods in such as a way as to entice customers to buy their goods by deceiving them into believing they are those of a competitor.

The test: the three fundamental elements of passing off are Reputation, Misrepresentation and Damage to goodwill. These three elements are also known as the Classical Trinity, as restated by the House of Lords in the case of *Reckitt & Colman Ltd V Borden INC* . It was stated in this case that in a suit for passing off the plaintiff must establish:

1. Goodwill or reputation attached to his goods or services.
2. They must prove a misrepresentation by the defendant to the public i.e. leading or likely to lead the public to believe that the goods and services offered by him are that of the plaintiffs.

---

[15] *Campomar Sociedad Limitada v Nike International Ltd*

3. They must demonstrate that he has suffered a loss due to the belief that the defendant's goods and services are those of the plaintiffs.

Passing Off

Elements of the Cause of Action

In the case of *Mc Cambridge ltd v Joseph Brennan Bakeries: 2012*: SCT: **Lord Oliver** said, as follows: *'no one may pass off his goods as those of another'.*[16]

Three stage test:

1. Goodwill (good name or reputation)

Goodwill means that the goods will have particular identifying features or something about them that will enable a reasonable person or a specific section of the general public to associate with those particular goods or services.

Some words and phrases cannot be copyrighted and the court held in *DSG Retail v PC World*, that common words or phrases will not be protected but unique spins on them will be, for instance the Acronym "PC" could not be protected but "PC World" could be.

2. Misrepresentation

There must be a false representation that will entice the reasonable person or general public to believe that the goods offered by the seller are in fact the goods or services of the other company. *Jameson v Irish Distillers:* The court held that the defendant was guilty of passing off despite using his own name.

3. Damage

This misrepresentation damages the goodwill of the claimant. That a reasonable person would have confused the two producers and the

---

[16] *In B&S Ltd. v. Irish Auto Trader Ltd. [1995] 2 I.R. 142 at 144, McCracken J. adopted the speech of Lord Diplock in Erven Warnink Bv. v J. Townend & Sons (Hull) [1979] A.C. 731 at p.742, as identifying the characteristics of passing off as:-*
(i) A misrepresentation,
(ii)made by a trader in the course of trade
(iii)to prospective customers of his or ultimate consumers of goods or services supplied by him
(iv)which is calculated to injure the business or goodwill of another trader (in the sense that it is a reasonably foreseeable consequence) and
(v)which causes actual damage to a business or goodwill of the trader by whom the action is brought or (in a quia timet action) will probably do so."

original producer brand would have suffered as loss as a consequence. Passing off is often connection with the production of counterfeit goods.

Domain Names

In order for a producer to protect their Domain names they must register the domain name as a trademark to ensure protection of their web address or homepage address.

Defence to "Passing Off"

If a seller or producer is producing in their own name with no malice or intent to misrepresent then this is a defence to PO

Remedies for "passing off"

Once an owner of a trademark registers the trademark with the Revenue Commissioners, they can report the infringement to the Garda, there may be an investigation and even a prosecution. Once the matter proceeds to Court, the Courts have the power to grant an injunction and/or the destruction of goods and damages. The Court can order destruction of the goods by An Garda Siochana

Defamation

Defamation is the false accusation or statement that is harmful to someone's reputation. The "tort of defamation" consists of the publication, by any means, of a defamatory statement about somebody to one or more person. A statement is not considered defamatory if it is published only to the person to whom it relates.

The original ***Defamation Act 1961*** states the definition of defamation was set out in case law. *McMahon and Binchy* define it as:

The wrongful publication of a false statement about a person, which tends to lower that person in the eyes of right-thinking members of society, or tends to hold that person up to hatred, ridicule or contempt, or causes that person to be shunned or avoided by right-thinking members of society.[17] Changes to this act did not occur until 2009, when a new defamation act was introduced and implemented the following year on January 1st, 2010. This new act allowed for new forms of defence for the press; however, journalists are still viewed as being guilty until proven otherwise.

The case must be taken within one year (two with special court permissions)

> ***Quigley V Creation*** = *if a certain amount of the community holds a negative view of the plaintiff due to the defamation of the defendant there is cause for action (able to sue)*
>
> ***Speight V Gosnay*** = *the original publisher is liable for republished materials even if they were not aware of the publication.*

Defences to Defamation.

Truth is normally an absolute defence.
The statement was privileged:
Absolute: judicial and legislative (Dáil/parliament) proceedings.
Qualified: said or printed in good faith, (limited defence).

---

[17] *Bryan McMahon & William Binchy, Irish Law of Torts 3rd Edition, (Dublin: Butterworths, 2000), 882.*

Defamation

Public Figures: plaintiff must show statement made with "actual malice."

Balance of rights

Article 40.6.1.i of the Irish Constitution says that the State guarantees the right of citizens to express freely their convictions and opinions. But the right of freedom of expression in Ireland is not absolute.[18]

In the 1988 case of ***Kennedy v Hearne***, the Irish High Court specifically acknowledged the role played by the law of defamation in vindicating a citizen's right to his good name.

A defamatory statement is only actionable if it is published. In the 1840 case of ***Ahern v Maguire[1840]***, Chief Baron Brady said that, if a letter *"however slanderous, is received only by the person to whom it is addressed, and does not go beyond him, there is no publication of it in law to support an action for libel".*[19]

A person who is aware that a libellous report is about to be published may apply to the courts for an injunction to prevent publication.

But in the case of ***National Irish Bank v Radio Telefís Éireann [1998]***[20]**,** the Supreme Court said that, if the publisher made out a strong case for publication on a public interest basis, the court, in its discretion, should not grant the injunction, but leaves the applicant to seek a remedy in damages.

[18] *The right of freedom of speech is also guaranteed by Article 10 (1) of the European Human Rights Convention. Article 10 (2) subjects this freedom to such restrictions "as are necessary in a democratic society in the interests of national security, territorial integrity or public safety, for the prevention of disorder or crime, for the protection of health or morals, for the protection of the reputation or rights of others, for preventing the disclosure of information received in confidence or for maintaining the authority and impartiality of the judiciary". Article 40.3.2 of the Constitution says "the State shall, in particular, by its laws, protect as best it may from unjust attack (and, in the case of injustice done, vindicate) the life, person, good name and property rights of every citizen."*

[19] *But a wrongly addressed letter containing defamatory remarks would be actionable if opened by someone other than the subject of the remarks.*

[20] *2 IR 465*

However, in 1998 the High Court granted an interlocutory injunction to nightclub owner John Reynolds to prevent former solicitor Elio Malocco publishing what Reynolds claimed would be a disparaging article about the club owner in a new magazine, *Patrick [1998]*[21].[22] Mr Justice Kelly said this *was "a jurisdiction of a delicate nature"* and *"the Court must be circumspect to ensure that it does not unnecessarily interfere with the right of freedom of expression".* A statement may be made orally or in writing, broadcast on radio or television or published on the internet, and includes electronic communications and visual images, sounds, gestures and any other method of signifying meaning.

Proof of special damage – or actual loss – is not required except actions for slander of title, slander of goods or malicious falsehood. The plaintiff must also prove that the statement was untrue, was published maliciously and referred to the plaintiff, his property or office, profession, calling, trade or business.

Where the plaintiff or defendant is making an allegation of fact, he must swear an affidavit verifying the allegations within two months of service of the pleadings. The maximum penalty for swearing a false or misleading affidavit is a fine of €50,000- and five-years' imprisonment. The defamation act applies to companies as well as individuals, and a company may bring a defamation action whether or not it has incurred any financial loss as a result. If the High Court award excessive awards there is a provision in section 13 that, on appeal, the Supreme Court may substitute an "appropriate amount of any High Court jury award".

Republication

Where a person/company republishes the defaming statements or story they are generally liable for those publications, there have been three situations where the courts have found in ***Speight V Gosnay (CA 1891***) that the republisher is liable to the same extent as the original publisher.

---

[21] *IEHC 175*

[22]*John Reynolds (plaintiff) v Elio Malocco trading as ["] Patrick["], Declan Murray, Frank White and Peter Laur and, by order, Fanville Limited (defendants).*

1. Where they authorise or intended the republication e.g. sending a letter to a newspaper

2. Where the person who republishes the words is under a legal or moral duty to repeat them to a third person.

3. Where the republication is the natural and probable result of the original publication.

Defamation Cases in Ireland

Talbot v. Hermitage Golf Club [2012][23]**.** Talbot was accused of handicap building and he made a claim for defamation which he lost, he claimed that the information was privileged. In July 1997, a jury awarded the former Government Minister, Proinsias de Rossa, damages of IR£300,000 (€380,921) for a libel in an Eamon Dunphy article published in the Sunday Independent in December 1992.[24], the *Sunday Independent* sought to challenge the system under Irish constitutional and defamation law whereby juries determine the size of the award without any realistic guidance by the trial judge.

They alleged that this procedure in practice leads to erratic and often excessive awards. In 1997, the Supreme Court had held in ***Dawson v Irish Brokers Association*** (Unreported, Supreme Court, 27 February 1997) that:

"Unjustifiably large awards, as well as the costs attendant on long trials, deal a blow to the freedom of expression entitlement that is enshrined in the Constitution"

In ***Sinclair v Gogarty 1937***[25], the plaintiffs sought an injunction restraining further publication of a book which contained imputations of sexual impropriety. In ***Green v. Blake (1948),*** a complaint was made against the owner of a horse which had run in a race. The complaint was investigated and the decision against the plaintiff, the owner, was published in the Racing Calendar. The court held that the publication was defamatory. In ***Kennedy v. Hearne (1988),*** allegations were made in court that a practising solicitor was a cheat and had no reputation[26]. Malocco Suggested that Reynolds tolerated the sale of drugs on his premises and was a "gay bachelor". ***McDonagh v.***

---

[23] *IEHC 372*

[24] *De Rossa -v- Independent Newspapers* [*1999*] 4 IR 432. The jury had decided that the article falsely alleged that Mr de Rossa was involved in or tolerated serious paramilitary crime, was anti-Semitic and supported violent communist oppression.

[25] *[1937] IR 377. Hanna J accepted that "sufficient indicia" in the passages to give readers the "necessary clue to their identity".*

[26] *Kennedy v Hearne, the Irish High Court specifically acknowledged the role played by the law of defamation in vindicating a citizen's right to his good name.*

Newsgroup. The defendant made a statement in the Sun paper stating that the Barrister was sympathetic to terrorists. The Supreme Court found this statement to be defamatory.

Identification

A defamatory statement need not necessarily name anyone. It may suggest a person or persons by - for example - their profession, location or connections. A former Garda commissioner was awarded £30,000 damages for the use of a graphic which featured his ears in a television programme on corruption[27]! If just one person gives credible evidence that he recognised the complainant by the description or image, which is enough to ground a defamation action. Only a false statement is actionable. But defamation differs from other torts in that a statement will be presumed to be defamatory until proved otherwise.[28]

[27] *Coleman v MNG Ltd [2012] IESC 20*

[28] *Rottman, D. Crime in the Republic of Ireland Rottman, D. (1980) Crime in the Republic of Ireland. Dublin: Economic and Social Research Institute*

Blasphemy (referendum in 2018 removed this from the DA 2010, as of December 2019)

Defamation Act 2010

Anyone who publishes or utters blasphemous matter shall be guilty of an offence and liable to a fine of up to €25,000.

Blasphemous matter is material that is *"grossly abusive or insulting"* about the beliefs held sacred by any religion[29], and which causes *"outrage among a substantial number of the adherents of that religion"*, where the defendant intends to cause such outrage. It is a defence to prove that a reasonable person would find *"genuine literary, artistic, political, scientific, or academic value in the matter to which the offence relates"*.

The court may issue a warrant to Gardaí to enter any premises (including a home), by force if necessary, at a *"reasonable" time*, where Gardaí have reasonable grounds for believing that copies of a blasphemous statement may be found.

The Gardaí may search the premises and seize and remove all copies of the statement found and may seize all copies of the statement in anyone's possession.

Remedies

(*Remedies are solutions to the problem*) A person who claims to be the subject of an alleged defamatory a statement may apply to the Circuit Court for a declaratory order that the statement is false and defamatory.

The court will make a declaratory order if it is satisfied that—

[29] "Religion" does not include an organisation whose principal object is making a profit, or an organisation that employs "oppressive psychological manipulation" of its followers, or to gain new followers.

- The respondent failed to do so or did not give the apology, correction or retraction similar prominence to the original statement.

Defences to Defamation

Defences

Defence of 'Truth'

Where a publisher proves that his statement is true in all material respects, then a claim will fail.

It is also not defamatory if published to another person, as long as:

- The publisher did not intend to publish the statement to the other person, and
- It was not reasonably foreseeable that publication to the first person would result in publication to the other person.

All earlier defences are abolished by the new act, except certain statutory defences. The main defence is now the defence of truth, where a defendant proves that his statement is true in all material respects.

The "honest opinion" defence is available for honestly-held opinions as long as—

- At the time of publication, the defendant believed in the truth of the opinion (or thought that its author believed it to be true),
- The opinion was based on proven (or honestly believed) allegations of fact that were known to those to whom the statement was published, or
- The opinion was based on proven (or reasonably likely) allegations of fact which were privileged, and the opinion related to a matter of public interest.

A person accused of defamation may make an offer of amends. Such an offer must be in writing and state:

- That it is an offer to make amends under section 22, and
- Whether it relates to the entire statement, part of it or a particular defamatory meaning only.

An offer to make amends cannot be made after the defence has been delivered. However, an offer may be withdrawn before it is accepted, and a new offer made.

An "offer to make amends" means an offer—

- To make a suitable correction and sufficient apology,
- To publish the correction and apology in a "reasonable and practicable" manner, and
- To pay agreed compensation, damages and costs.

If an offer to make amends is accepted and the parties agree on the implementation of the offer, the court may direct the defendant to take those measures. If the parties do not agree, the person who made the offer may make a correction and apology in a statement before the court in terms approved by the court and give an undertaking about the manner of publication.

One important change in the new act is that an apology no longer constitutes an express or implied admission of liability and is not relevant to the issue of liability.

The defence of consent may be pleaded where a plaintiff consented to publication of the impugned statement. The defence of innocent publication may be pleaded where the defendant can prove that—

- He was not the author, editor or publisher of the statement,
- He took reasonable care in relation to its publication and
- He did not know, and had no reason to believe, that his actions would lead to defamation proceedings

Privilege

If a statement is privileged, a potential plaintiff has no cause of action. There are two types of privilege: absolute privilege and qualified privilege. In the case of absolute privilege, the intentions of the publisher are irrelevant. For example, a Dáil deputy or a member of the Seanad may say what he wishes about a person within the confines of the chamber. No matter how scurrilous the allegation or how improper the motive for making it, he may not be sued for that statement.

A fair, accurate and contemporaneous media report of Oireachtas or court proceedings is also absolutely privileged, even if the reporter is motivated by malice.

Qualified Privilege

Qualified privilege may be pleaded as a defence where a statement was published to a person who had a legal, moral or social duty to receive the information, or where the defendant reasonably believed that the person had such a duty or interest, and the defendant had a corresponding duty to communicate the information.

The defence of qualified privilege fails if the plaintiff proves malice. However, the defence will not fail just because the statement was published to someone else by mistake.

Where a defence of qualified privilege fails in the case of one defendant, another defendant may still plead that defence unless he was vicariously liable for the acts or omissions of the first defendant which led to the publication.

Defamation in the Information age

The European E-Commerce Directive (2003/31/EU) states under article 12 that Internet service providers will not be liable for defamatory material transmitted on their sites, provided they:

- Do not initiate the transmission, select the recipient or modify the information contained in it.
- Under article 14, they will not be required to monitor content, but if defamatory matter on it is brought to their attention, they will be required to remove it.

ISP Service Providers

Section 23 of The Electronic Commerce Act 2000, states that all provisions of existing defamation law shall apply to all electronic communications within the state.

Regulation 16 of the European E-Commerce Directive (2003/31/EU) states:

An intermediary service provider shall not be liable for information transmitted by him or her in a communication network if –

a) The information has been provided to him or her by a recipient of a relevant service provided by him or her (being a service consisting of the transmission in a communication network of that information), or

b) A relevant service provided by him or her consist of the provision of access to a communication network, and, in either case, the following conditions are complied with –

i. The intermediary service provider did not initiate the transmission,

ii. The intermediary service provider did not select the receiver of the transmission, and

iii. The intermediary service provider did not select or modify the information contained in the transmission.

To date, there have been relatively few emails and Internet defamation cases in Ireland. The reason for which may have been the "uncertain state of the law, difficulties in identifying authors of cyberspace defamations, and question marks over the potential liability for employers for e-mail abuse by those who work for them." But with the 2009 reform of the Defamation Act, and over 2,830,000, Internet users in Ireland and counting, litigation is likely to increase.[30]

Blogger settles €100,000 lawsuit for Defamation

A statement posted on a blog in 2006 has resulted in a €100,000 pay-out to the two people who were defamed in the statement. The blogger who writes a diary type blog made a remark about Niall Ó Donnchú, a senior civil servant, and his girlfriend Laura Barnes.

Barnes, an American book dealer had sold the James Joyce original papers to the Irish Government. Ardmayle posted a comment about the couple and the sale of the Joycean manuscripts under the headline "Barnes and Noble". The couple made separate suits against the blogger and the couple's solicitor Ivor Fitzpatrick solicitors received an apology from the blogger retracting his remarks and apologising for the remarks.

X factor judge Louis Walsh has settled over the sun newspaper[31] *published an article claimed that Mr Walsh has sexually assaulted Leonard Watters in a Dublin night club. The out of court settlement was for 500,000 euro (£403,500) was paid by News Group Newspapers in Ireland.*

---

[30] *Internet World Stats, 2010, 'Internet Usage in Europe: Internet User Statistics & Population for 53 European Countries and Regions', www.internetworldstats.com, accessed: 2nd November 2012*
[31] *Louis Walsh v News Group Newspapers [2012]*

Defamation Damages

Damages

Damages in a defamation case may be high enough to put a media organisation out of business - even before considering the matter of legal costs.

General Damages.

When an injured party succeeds in proving defamation the jury may award damages as compensation for the injury caused.

Special Damages

An injured party may recover special damages if actual financial losses can be proved, for example, if the claimant lost his job as a result of the publication.

Aggravated Damages

The jury may award aggravated damages if the defendant aggravated the injury to the claimant in the conduct of its defence.

Punitive Damages

Where a publisher who is shown to have intended to publish the defamatory statement recklessly or knowing that the statement was untrue, the jury may award punitive damages.

Win or lose

A defendant who loses a defamation action is likely to have to meet the legal bill of both sides. He may limit his exposure to costs by lodging money in court in an offer of settlement. The highest award ever given by an Irish court in defamation was €10 million in November 2010. The award was made to businessman Donal Kinsella, who sued his former employer, Kenmare Resources, over a press release it sent out concerning an incident where he had sleepwalked into a woman's bedroom while on company business in Africa. Prior to the Kinsella case, the highest libel award was €1.9 million in damages awarded to

Defamation Damages

Mrs Monica Leech over a series of articles in the Evening Herald newspaper in 2004 which falsely suggested that she had had an affair with a government minister, If a publisher pleads justification *(that an alleged fact is substantially true*) and this turns out not to be the case, the jury may award aggravated damages as a punishment for the additional harm done to the complainant's reputation.[32] Since the establishment of the Press Ombudsman and the Press Council of Ireland in 2007, anyone who believes he or she has been defamed may complain to the Press Ombudsman.[33]

Injunctions

- mandatory injunction (make defendant do something)
- prohibitory injunction (stop the defendant doing something)
- interim (temporary)
- interlocutory (an order while awaiting the outcome of an interim order)
- perpetual (a permanent injunction)

---

[32] For example, when Elton John sued the Sunday Mirror in 1993, he was awarded £75,000 in ordinary damages, but almost four times that amount in punitive damages. (This was reduced to a total of £75,000 on appeal.) April 2001 case of Irish parliamentarian Beverley Cooper-Flynn against state broadcaster RTE, the jury found that RTE had not proved its case, but other evidence showed that the plaintiff's character had not been damaged. She was awarded no damages and ordered to pay a legal bill estimated at £2 million.

Unintentional Torts

Negligence

Negligence is the most important field of tort law as it governs most activities of modern society. For a successful claim in negligence the plaintiff must prove on a balance of probabilities, then following four elements, which are discussed below in detail:

1. Duty: the defendant owed a duty of care to the injured party
2. Breach: the defendant breached the duty of care owed
3. Causation: the breach caused the damage suffered by the injured party

In a nutshell, to establish negligence, "A, B and C's" of negligence must be shown, such as:

a) A duty of care must exist between the person injured and the person responsible for that injury;

b) Conduct of the defendant fell short of that duty of care; and

c) Resulting in damage to another person.

Negligence occurs when the defendant's conduct that falls below the standards of behaviour established by law for the protection of others against unreasonable risk of harm. A person has acted negligently if he or she has departed from the conduct expected of a reasonably prudent person acting under similar circumstances.

For example: *it must be proved that you owed the person claiming against you a duty to take care, to ensure your actions didn't hurt them.*

Then it must be proved that the defendant didn't take care when they were going about their business and their carelessness or recklessness hurt the other person, and finally it must be proved that the defendant's lack of care or carelessness or recklessness was the cause of the other person's injuries.

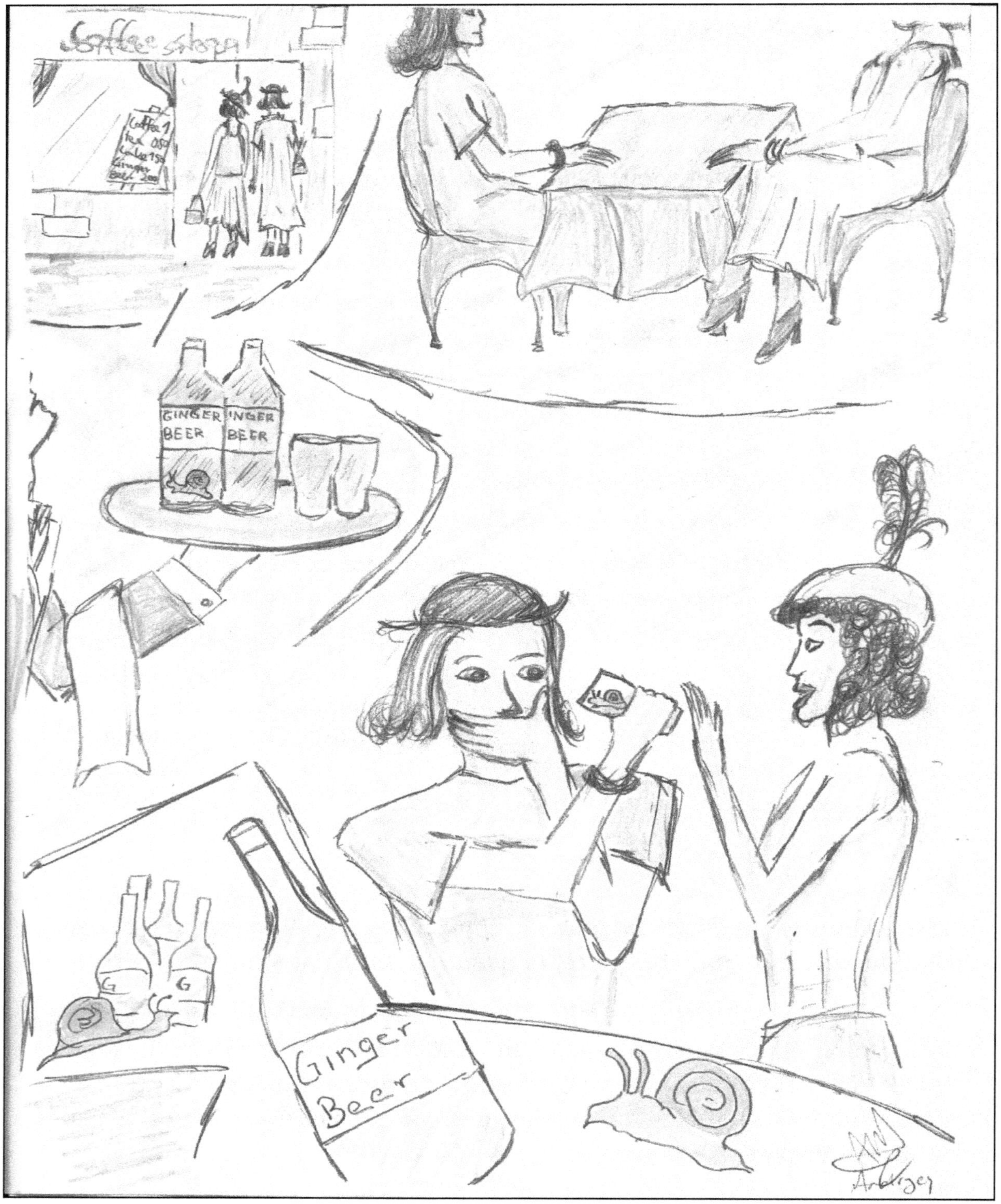
Coffee shop
GINGER BEER
INGER BEER
G
G
Ginger Beer

Duty of Care

A duty of care was originally established by applying Lord Atkin's "*Neighbour*"[34] Test from: ***Donoghue v Stevenson (1932).***[35] Mrs Donoghue was a bottle of bought ginger beer by her friend, and she drank the beer, she realised when she got near the bottom there was a decomposing snail in the bottle (*bottles in those days were ceramic, and therefore she could not see until she got to the end*), because of this she suffered shock and gastroenteritis. Mrs Donoghue had no action against the shop owner, she had no contract with them), he had not been negligent in any way (he had not bottled the ginger beer, only sold it). The question was then, could she take an action against the manufacturer of the ginger beer[36]. The Court ruled in her favour, finding that a duty of care was owed to your 'neighbour'.

Duty of care

This is the duty owed by one person to another, we must prove that there is a duty (a requirement to take care), or it can be automatic as in parent child, employer employee,

Donoghue v Stevenson = *you must take care that your actions do not affect your neighbour, (proximity and foreseeability)* ***Caparo Industries v. Dickman Plc*** = *same as above 1) proximity and 2) foreseeability PLUS also 3) fair, just and reasonable.*

Lord Aiken stated that:

"The rule that you must love your neighbour becomes in law you must not injure your neighbour; and the lawyer's question, who is my neighbour, receives a restricted reply. You must take reasonable care to avoid acts or omissions which you can reasonably foresee would be liable to injure your neighbour. Who, then, in law, is my neighbour? The answer seems to be - persons who are so closely and directly affected by my act that I ought reasonably to have them in contemplation as being so affected

---

[34] *The 'neighbour principle' by Lord Atkin in Donoghue v Stevenson [1932] A.C. 562*

[35] *Mrs Donoghue was unable to take a case for breach of contract due to the fact that her friend had bought the ginger beer for her, she was not "privy" to the contract and therefore had to find an alternative way to seek redress (compensation etc.), this was set the precedent of "take care not to injure your neighbour, a neighbour being anyone directly affected by your actions"*

Illustration on Donoghue v Stevenson by Margret Hagan http://www.margarethagan.com/wp-content/uploads/2013/03/razblint-illustrated-law-school-nuisance-am-i-one.png

when I am directing my mind to the acts or omissions which are called in question."

In, ***Ward v McMaster, Louth County Council and Nicholas Hardy & Co. Ltd. [1985]***[37], it was held that the duty of care arose from the proximity (*nearness or closeness space or time, a contract or a relationship*) of the parties and the foreseeability (*would a reasonable person have foreseen it*) of the damage, balanced against the "absence of any compelling exemption based upon public policy (*in the public's best interest*[38])

However, The Supreme Court however does seem to be reverting to the UK approaches such as in ***Purtill v Athlone UDC [1968] I.R. 205***, the Supreme Court dealt with a case where a young boy had entered an abattoir, the doors of the abattoir were not closed nor rarely were, the boy had access to the building, he gained access as did many other local children, the boy got his hands on a detonators which was used in the pistols to slaughter the animals, the boy took detonators from the abattoir on several occasions and exploded them either in his back garden at home or in the garden, a detonator hit him in the eye and resulted in the loss of his right eye.

The abattoir was sued by the boy for negligence. The abattoir claimed that as he was a trespasser and they did not owe him a duty of care. Foreseeability was also considered as the defendants claimed that the loss suffered was too remote (not foreseeable by a reasonable person, *too far away from the original incident*) for them to be liable there claiming he had contributed to his injuries.

The Supreme Court rejected the claim of trespass and focused on whether a duty of care existed. The court established that there was "***proximity***" as they local boys were regularly in the abattoir and owed a duty by the abattoir and employees also, that it was foreseeable that if a

---

[37] *Ward v McMaster, Louth County Council and Nicholas Hardy & Co. Ltd. [1985] I.R. 29*

[38] *i.e. fire engine or ambulance going through a red light and hitting a car, the court would look to see if the god they were trying to achieve overweighed the damage they caused, i.e. your car got a dent, but they were going to a house fire with 10 people trapped, the court may take the opinion that your bit of damage was not as important as saving the lives of the ten people."*

boy were to get their hands on a detonator by simply walking through the gates and then through the doors that they may be severely injured, "***foreseeability***" and therefore the boy was owed a "***duty of care***".

Walsh J, stated that *"When the danger is reasonably foreseeable, the duty to take care to avoid injury to those who are proximate, when their proximity is known ... is based upon the duty that one man has to those in proximity to him to take reasonable care that they are not injured by his acts."*

The Court accepted that the plaintiff had contributed to his own injuries and a 15% liability was imposed on him.

Historical development regarding the duty of care in England and Wales

The **Caparo**, modern or the "*Three Stage Test*"

The House of Lords refined the neighbour test further, as follows:

i. There must be sufficient proximity;

ii. The harm must have been reasonably foreseeable;

iii. The imposition of a duty must be fair, just and reasonable in the circumstances.

This approach is virtually identical to the two-stage test (difference = proximity and foreseeability are separated out, and the neutral language removes the pro-plaintiff slant). The third test has often been criticised, as this policy is already used to apply stages (i) and (ii), thus rendering the third limb moot.

The duty of care was further extended in ***Caparo Industries PLC v Dickman [1990].*** This case imposed a further requirement on proving a duty of care exists, whether in all the circumstances it would be fair, just and reasonable that the law should impose a duty.

Lord Bridge said:

"What emerges is that, in addition to the foreseeability of damage, the necessary ingredients in any situation giving rise to a duty of care are that there should exist between the party owing the duty and the party to whom it is owed a relationship characterised by the law as one of 'proximity' or 'neighbourhood' and that the situation should be one in which the court considers it fair, just and reasonable that the law should impose a duty of a given scope upon the one party for the benefit of the other..."

Irish development in duty of care

Glencar had a mining licence; Mayo County Council put in motion a development plan banning mining, rendering the Glencar's licence obsolete. Court held that Mayo County Council had acted Ultra Vires. However, the High Court and subsequently the Supreme Court dismissed the claims of Glencar, stating although Mayo Co Council was negligent, this did not give rise to a breach of duty and their claim for compensation was dismissed.

Keane CJ dealt with the duty of care and the neighbour principle. He was unsure if the two-step test of **Anns case**[39] was the correct test to follow in this case and further discussed the decision of the Ward case. He stated that: "There is, in my view, no reason why courts determining whether a duty of care arises should consider themselves obliged to hold that it does in every case where injury or damage to property was reasonably foreseeable, and the notoriously difficult and elusive test of 'proximity' or 'neighbourhood' can be said to have been met, unless very powerful public policy considerations dictate otherwise. It seems to me that no injustice will be done if they are required to take the further step of considering whether, in all the circumstances, it is just and

[39] ***Anns v Merton*** - *The local authority failed to ensure building work correctly followed the plans, resulting in shallow foundations. The Anns test reformed: 1) is there a relationship of proximity so that damage is reasonably foreseeable? 2) are there any other considerations to not make the Defendant liable. This case brought together the two tests of foreseeability and proximity. As the builders went into liquidation the only avenue open to the claimant was to sue the local authority. Lord Wilberforce's verdict and 2-tier test developed some areas of law significantly, such as pure economic loss and nervous shock. This was a very controversial test and was soon replaced.*

reasonable that the law should impose a duty of a given scope on the defendant for the benefit of the plaintiff ..." The judgment in this case added a third step to the Anns test. As with Caparo, the court asked, "Is it just and reasonable to impose a duty of care on the Defendant".

Foreseeability and Policy Factors

The second element of the duty of care is reasonable foreseeability that the Plaintiff would suffer damage due to carelessness by the Defendant. The Courts will use policy factors to decide on what is foreseeable in the circumstances by reference to public expectation in particular. The Courts are also anxious to ensure that foreseeability alone is not used to determine liability but must be considered where a proximate relationship exists. Otherwise liability could be imposed on a wide range of Defendants where it was foreseeable that a stranger would suffer injury or harm.

Contributory Negligence

In many incidents where loss occurs, both parties may have, by their negligence, contributed to the loss. At common law, it was generally the case that if the plaintiff was to blame for the accident, he would receive no damages. Since 1961, by virtue of the ***Civil Liability Act 1961***, where a person suffers loss partly as a result of their own fault, and partly due to the fault of another, the damages recoverable will be reduced according to the share of the responsibility.[40] In ***Sinnot v. Quinnsworth (1984),*** the plaintiff was a passenger in a car owned by the defendant and was injured in a collision with a bus. Evidence showed that the injuries would have been less serious if the plaintiff had been wearing a seat belt. The Court did accept, however, that the plaintiff had contributed to his own injuries and a 15% liability was apportioned to him.[41]

---

[40] *S.34 of the Act provides that where it is not possible to establish different degrees of fault, the liability will be apportioned equally.*

[41] *S.34 (2)(b) of the Civil Liability Act provides that a negligent or careless failure to mitigate damage (reduce your own damage) can also be deemed to be contributory negligence in respect of the amount by which such damage exceeds the damage that otherwise would have occurred.*

The Standard of Care

When a Defendant is found to owe a duty of care to a Plaintiff, he/she will be subject to a standard of care. The standard is that of a "***Reasonable Man***". If the Defendant's conduct falls short of the standard of care, which he owed in the circumstances of the case, he is said to have breached his duty of care to the Plaintiff, i.e. not acted the way a reasonable person would have. ***Collins v Mid-Western Health Board [1999] IESC 73***

The court held that a GP cannot be expected to have the same expertise as a consultant or specialist; however, s/he should be aware when it is necessary to take appropriate specialist advice.

For example: *a reasonable driver will put their seat belt on, ensure that their car has insurance and pay attention to the road and safety, they will also know the rules of the road. An unreasonable driver might have no seat belt, be driving while drunk and using their mobile phone while driving on bald tyres.*

Breach (of the duty of care)

> ***Breach*** *(standard)*
>
> *If you do owe a duty and hurt your neighbour the court will see if you acted like a reasonable person would, would a person with your skills and qualifications and experience had done that, (reach above or fall below that standard),*

Once it has been established (shown or recognised) that the defendant owe a duty to take care in their daily life to this person or people, then it must be established that the defendant have breached that duty, (prove they acted negligently or recklessly), that the defendant acts or omissions were not that of a reasonable person in their position.

The breach of a legal duty to take care; results in damage to the claimant which was not desired by the defendant. Per Alderson B., *"Negligence is the omission to do something which a reasonable man, guided upon those considerations which ordinarily regulate the conduct of human affairs, would do, or doing something which a prudent and reasonable man would not do."* [42]

Negligence and the "reasonable dog" standard? (an actual case from the USA)

November 21st, 2011

Would a reasonably prudent dog batter a postal worker, negligently knock over a vase with a wagging tail or trespass on property to urinate or defecate?

Maybe we'll find out, now that a court has held that a dog in a dog-bite case was to be judged by a "reasonable dog" standard.

In *Kirkham v. Will,* an Illinois intermediate appellate court held that, in deciding whether the defence of provocation applied in a dog-bite case, the appropriate test to apply was the "reasonable dog" standard; that is, how a reasonable dog would have reacted to the plaintiff's presence under similar circumstances.

We entrust the decision to jurors because they presumably know how reasonable people would act. Are they competent to determine how reasonable dogs would act? I can see it now, ads for expert witnesses in "Canine Behaviour."

— *Kirkham v. Will,* 724 N.E.2d 1062, 1065 (Ill. App. Ct. 2000).

---

[42] *Blyth v Birmingham Waterworks Co. (1856)*

Causation

Causation

The claimant must prove that the breach of duty caused, or substantially contributed to, the damage suffered. In ***the Wagon Mound 2 (1961)*** a ship's crew had carelessly allowed furnace oil to leak from their ship. The oil drifted under a wharf and thickly coating both the water and the shore, where other ships were being repaired. Hot metal produced by welders using oxyacetylene torches on the wharf ignited the oil on the water. This resulted in substantial fire damage to the wharf and the ship moored there. In relation to the resulting claim for damages;

Causation

This means did your behaviour cause the damage to the other person; (did your actions fall below the standard of a reasonable person you owed a duty to take care to?)

- the court stated that the crewmen did not know and could not reasonably have been expected to
- know that the oil was capable of being set alight when spread on water, and therefore could not
- be liable for all losses incurred.

Causes-in-fact

"Cause in fact" is a question of fact to establish a causal link between the incident and the injury.

Tests to establish causation

1. "But for" test
2. The chain of causation test
3. Was there a Novus Actus Interveniens?
4. The material contribution test
5. Bolitho test for omissions
6. Fairchild

Causation

The "but for" Test

First, the basic test for determining causation remains the "but for" test. This applies to multi cause injuries. The plaintiff bears the burden of showing that "but for" the negligent act or omission of each defendant, the injury would not have occurred. Having done this, contributory negligence may be apportioned, as permitted by statute.

Example: But for (if it was not for) the defendants actions would the plaintiff have suffered the loss or damage?.. *This is the test for proximity, causation; in plain English it can be explained as, is the Defendant the material cause of the damage, or was the Defendant the biggest cause of the damage, we can see in* ***Barnett v Chelsea*** *(below) the but for test in action, the court asked "but for" the doctors actions, would the patient have died. In this case it means was the hospital the cause of the man's death? no, he would have died anyway, the poison was untreatable, the hospital may have had a duty of care, "yes", and breached that duty "yes", but did they cause the man's death, "no", therefore no causation is proven and case fails. So, in Barnett case the "but for" test basically asked was the hospital the main "material" case of death.*

In ***Barnett v Chelsea & Kensington Hospital (1969)*** three night watchmen drank tea and began to vomit. They attended casualty, where they were told by the nurse to go home. One man died from arsenic poisoning three hours later. The court held that although the hospital was in breach of their duty to care, in that a doctor did not see, examine, admit or treat the patient, the breach did not cause the death of the man. The man would not have recovered from the poisoning, even if he had been treated by a doctor.

Novus Actus Interveniens

(*New act which occurs*) Did any act or omission occur from the breach to the damage, there is a car crash, two cars, one pulled out in front of the other, then a third car crashed into them, one passenger died, question, was it the first or second car who was the cause of the death? If it was the second car then no Actus Interveniens, if it was the third then the second car is not fully liable.

If the defendant's act merely provided the setting in which some other cause operated, the chain of causation would be broken.

Material Contribution test

In ***McGhee v National Coal Board (1973)*** a man who was exposed to brick dust in his employment for a considerable period of time developed dermatitis. His wife brought an action for negligence against his employers. The court held that there were a number of factors that led to his injury but one of them was the failure by the employers to provide washing facilities. Although this was not the sole cause of the injury, it materially increased the risk of injury and therefore the employers were held to be liable in negligence.

For example: *the person causing the damage will not have to pay all the compensation for all damages but the amount they will have to pay will depend on how much of a contribution they made to the damage.*

Bolitho Test

A test that modified the 1957 Bolam test which the British courts had used to determine medical negligence, by a doctor or nurse. ***In Bolitho v. City and Hackney Health Authority, 1997***. The Bolitho test requires that the medical professional who allegedly carried out the medical negligence be found to have been unreasonable. A doctor or specialist needs to have acted outside the behaviour of a reasonable and competent medical professional. **For example:** *they should only act the way a reasonable doctor would.*

Fairchild

In ***Fairchild v Glenhaven Funeral Services & Ors [2003] 1 AC 32***, employees had developed mesothelioma from exposure to asbestos dust while at work, but there was uncertainty as to which of several employers was responsible for the exposure which had caused the disease. The court found where there had been exposure by different employers, but the precise instrumental cause could not be identified, that this was enough to find them all contributors.

Remoteness of Damages

Remoteness

Remoteness (*remote is foreseeable by a reasonable and prudent person, too remote means unforeseeable by a reasonable and prudent person*), this involves fixing a cut-off point beyond which the defendant will no longer be liable for damage done to the plaintiff. The remoteness issue limits the extent of the defendant's liability.[43]

> ***Remoteness***
>
> *If you did owe a duty and you did breach that duty and your actions fell below those of a reasonable person, was that damage cause reasonably foreseeable (would you have ever thought that could have happened, i.e. I never thought in a million years that would happen.)*

For example: *If a person was to go out driving on a frosty and icy day them it is remote or foreseeable that their car might skid or slide into a verge or path, or even another car, however, say the car is in the foreseeable and remote skid and there is an old lady looking out of her bedroom window, she sees the car skid and sees a child with their back to the car, she fears that the car will hit the child, she opened the window to lean out to shout and warn the child and slips and falls out the window. The court will have to look and see if the driver is liable for the old ladies' injuries. It is very likely that the court will not find the driver liable for her injuries as it was too remote, or completely unforeseeable that she would have fallen out the window of her house just because he was having a skid on the road, therefore* ***too remote*** *and completely* ***unforeseeable****, you could also define it as:* ***I wouldn't have dreamt of that in a million years****..!*

"Cause in law"

The extent of the defendant's liability is determined by the boundaries set by the judges. The defendant is only liable for damage that is of a kind which is reasonably foreseeable. It is up to the courts define the type of damage.

---

[43] ***Re Polemis****: the court looked at the principle of foreseeable damages, was the damage as a direct consequences, in this case a spark had ignited oil on the water destroying the entire ship*
The Wagon Mound: *this case set the precedent for reasonably foreseeability, this states that the plaintiff: can only recover for damage that is reasonably foreseeable.*

The "thin skull" rule.

The 'thin skull' rule says that the defendant must take his victim as he finds him. Therefore, even if injury or death is not reasonably foreseeable the law still considers the defendant liable if the victim suffered from any physical or mental condition that made him or her vulnerable. It is called the 'thin skull rule' in appreciation that if the defendant knocks a person to the ground who has such a skull, the defendant should be liable. It is not the victim's fault that he was not blessed with a more substantial cranium.

For Example: *If a person has sight in only one eye and is working in a dangerous job, the job required goggles but the employer does not provide or supply goggles, say for instance that the employee damages their good eye because they had no goggles and are no blind, the employer might fight the case by saying they only damaged one eye and therefore they are not responsible for the blindness, they court will normally take the view that they employer should take the employee as they find them and therefore a knowing they were blind in one eye should have taken extra precaution to ensure the safety of the remaining eye and therefore liable for the blindness.*

The damage suffered by Plaintiff must not be too remote. In other words, the Defendant may not necessarily be liable for all the consequences of his negligence. The concept of remoteness is concerned with fixing "a cut-off" point beyond which the Defendant will not be liable for damage suffered by P.

Original UK Approach

Re Polemis [1921][44]

This defendant who was found to be at fault was held to be liable for all of the direct consequences of his action

---

[44] *Re Polemis [1921] 3 KB 560*

Remoteness of Damages

Current Irish and UK Approach

Reasonable foreseeability test

Once the injury is sustained by Plaintiff and it is reasonably foreseeable, it does not matter that it is, in fact, more serious than could reasonably have been foreseen by defendant.

For example: *one you have suffered damage or injury by the other party, it is irrelevant that you broke your two legs when he would have thought you would only have gotten a scratch.*

Professional Negligence

The Tort of professional negligence comprises a subset of the general rules of negligence. The general situation covered by professional negligence is a situation in which the Defendant has represented himself or herself as having more than average skills and abilities. By virtue of the services, which they offer and supply, professional people regard themselves out as having more than average abilities.

Generally speaking, the occupations regarded as professions have four particular characteristics:

- The work or service is skilled and specialised;
- The practitioner is expected to provide a high standard of service and is expected to be
- particularly concerned about the duty of confidentiality;
- Practitioners usually belong to a professional association which regulates admission and seeks
- to uphold the standards of the profession;
- The practitioner holds a high status in the community.

<u>Professional duty of care</u>, *this is where a professional in their job is held to have a higher standard than a layperson, therefore higher standard of professional duty of care, i.e. a doctors stops at an accident and the patent dies, good Samaritan laws protect an ordinary citizen who stops to try and help, whereas a doctor merely driving by "off duty" will still be held to the professional standard of care.*

The definition of "profession" was stated in one case to be as follows: -

"A "profession" in the present use of language involves the idea of an occupation requiring either purely intellectual skill, or of manual skill controlled, as in painting and sculpture, or surgery, by the intellect of the operator as distinguished from an occupation which is substantially the production or sale or arrangements for the production or sale of commodities. The line of demarcation may vary from time to time. The word "profession" used to be confined to the three learned professions, the church, medicine and law. It has now, I think, a wider meaning". The law of professional negligence has developed to include as part of the meaning of the term "profession" much more than simply doctors, lawyers and religious. The law relating to professional negligence has been developed to include the likes of architects, engineers, quantity surveyors, insurance brokers and accountants, amongst other professions.

Defences in Negligence

- Inevitable accident
- Voluntary assumption of risk (defence of consent)
- Illegality
- Contributory Negligence

Voluntary assumption of risk (defence of consent)

Where the plaintiff has willingly placed themselves in a position where they may cause harm to themselves or where the reasonable person would be aware that the action carries a risk. The court must be able to satisfy that the plaintiff was free to agree or not agree. It has two main elements:

- The claimant was fully aware of all the risks involved

AND

- The claimant expressly (by statement) or implicitly (by actions) consented to waive all claims for damages

Morris v Murray 1991 – both parties had been drinking all day, the defendant, who had a pilot licence and a light aircraft suggested that they took the aircraft for a flight. The claimant agreed and drove them both to the airfield. Shortly after take-off they crashed. The Defendant was killed, and the claimant was seriously injured. The Defence was allowed. The actions of the Claimant in accepting a ride in an aircraft from an obviously heavily intoxicated pilot was so glaringly dangerous that he could be taken to have voluntarily accepted the risk of injury and waived the right to compensation.

Regan v Irish Automobile Club 1990 – the court ruled that the plaintiff could not make a claim for damages because she had consented to the to the risk involved by accepting the job as flag martial at a car race and had signed a contract before she commenced employment.

Illegality

When the plaintiff knowingly engaged in an illegal activity at the time the injury occurred the defendant can use this defence. The right for damages is reduced if this occurs. Cases used to understand this form of defence are

Cumming v Granger 1971 – a guard dog bit a burglar, the burglar was prohibited from claiming for damages because the injuries he sustained were while he was preforming an illegal activity

Revill v Newbergy 1996 - On hearing the plaintiff trying to break in, he shot his gun through a hole in the shed, injuring the plaintiff. At first instance, the judge awarded damages on the basis that the defendant had used violence in excess of the reasonable. On appeal it was held the Claimants action was successful, but his damages were reduced by 2/3 under the Law Reform (Contributory Negligence) Act 1945 to reflect his responsibility for his own injuries.

Contributory Negligence

Under the *Civil Liability Act 1961* contributory negligence is a partial defence, which enables the defendant's liability to be reduced if the plaintiff has somehow contributed to his own injuries. The court will examine the contribution of both parties to the injuries sustained and apportion the percentage of responsibility to each party.

The case used to understand this form of defence are

Jones v Livox Quarries 1952 – the plaintiff got injured while travelling on the tow bar of a vehicle which is prohibited, and he did not inform the driver either. The Defendants liability was reduced because of the Plaintiffs actions. The Plaintiff exposed himself to the risk of injury and therefore his compensation was reduced because of his own behaviour.

Types of losses in Negligence

Remedies in Negligence

Damages

Nominal - defendant has committed a tort, but the claimant has suffered no loss. **Contemptuous**, means you win, but you shouldn't have brought this case, award could be 1 cent.

Special = can be calculated, i.e. wages, doctors, etc.

General = cannot be (easily) calculated, such as pain and suffering.

Aggravated = actions which further shock the plaintiff, and

Exemplary = shocked the court.

Injunctions

- mandatory injunction (make defendant do something)
- prohibitory injunction (stop the defendant doing something)
- interim (temporary)
- interlocutory (an order while awaiting the outcome of an interim order)
- perpetual (a permanent injunction)

Types of losses

Pecuniary losses:

(Quantifiable) Ascertainable or possibly agreed amounts of money

Non pecuniary losses

(Unknown amounts of money) will have to be defined by court.

Liquidated damages

Damages which are agreed before the contract is formed, i.e. a set amount that will be paid if the contract is breached or the terms not adhered to.

Types of losses in Negligence

Unliquidated damages

Amounts of money which cannot be foreseen or assessed, the judge will assed and decide.

Strict Liability Torts

1. *Occupiers Liability*
2. *Vicarious Liability*
3. *Liability for defective Products Act 1991*
4. *Rylands v. Fletcher (strict Liability in the tort of nuisance)*

The Occupiers Liability Act 1995

An occupier is defined as a person exercising such control over the state of the premises that it is reasonable to impose upon that person a duty towards an entrant in respect of a particular danger thereon.

The defining characteristic of the occupier is the element of control over the premises in question. It is not required that the occupier own the premises, merely that sufficient control be exercised by him over the premises that it is reasonable to impose a duty upon him, or phrased differently, that the degree of control is such that the person ought to realise that a failure on his part may cause injury to an entrant. A useful yardstick is whether the person in question has authority to admit or exclude persons from the premises. Equally, the control exercised must be more than merely tenuous control. In ***Keegan -V- Owens and McMahon***, a community of nuns were found not to be occupiers of a field because although they had permission to use, and had promoted a carnival thereon, the management and running of the carnival was controlled by a working committee.

Premises include, land, water, and any fixed or moveable structures thereon, and also includes vessels, vehicles, trains, aircraft, and other means of transport.

Employers Liability

Vicarious Liability

(This happens when a person is held responsible for the actions or omissions of another person)

Vicarious Liability

The liability of one person (principal/employer) for actions of another person (agent/employee), who was acting on principal's behalf.

In negligence cases, most often involves employers and employees or principals and agents. The employer is responsible for torts committed by employees while at work and ACTING on the employer's instructions

The doctrine of Vicarious Liability imposes responsibility upon one person for the failure of another, with whom the person has a special relationship (such as Parent and Child, employer and employee, or owner of vehicle and driver), to exercise such care as a reasonably prudent person would use under similar circumstances. An editor may be held responsible for the actions of their staff, reporters, journalists etc., and an employer may be held responsible for the actions of an employee if they defamed another person as part of their employment contract.

The most common example is where an employee is guilty of negligence which results in injury to a third party such as a customer. That third party may take legal action against the employer in such circumstances. The reason behind this was outlined by in ***Majrowski - v- Guy's and St Thomas' NHS Trust [2006]***[45] as follows: (Ireland, 2012)

- The employer is in control of the employee's actions

[45]*U.K.H.L. 34, [2006] I.R.L.R. 695*

- The employee would not have been in a position to commit the wrongdoing, but for the fact that s/he was carrying out the employer's activities
- The employer is usually in a better position to absorb the financial loss of a civil claim (e.g. liability insurance, ability to increase prices to absorb liability)
- Vicarious liability ensures that employers promote good practice and train employees properly in terms of working practices and health and safety.

Moynihan v Moynihan [1975]

The plaintiff, a two year old child was scalded by a teapot which was left unattended by the defendant's daughter (child's aunt), the grandmother had asked the aunt to pour the tea, when she had poured the tea, she left the room and left the child unattended with the hot teapot, **HELD:** The court held that the Grandmother was vicariously liable, as her instructions were an express delegation as the hospitality had been completely under her control. [46]

Employers Liability

An employer will only be liable for an employee's wrongdoings where it can be established that those wrongdoings occurred during the course of employment.

Smith -v- Stages [1989][47] as "an employee [who] is acting in the course of his employment when he is doing what he is employed to do...

[46] *Moynihan v. Moynihan [1975] IR 192 (Walsh J)."This power of control was not in any way dependent upon the relationship of mother and daughter but upon the relationship of the head of a household with a person to whom some of the duties of the head of the household had been delegated by that head. The position would be no different, therefore, from that of a case where the head of a household had requested a neighbour to come in and assist in the giving of a dinner-party because she had not any, or not sufficient, hired domestic help. It would produce a strange situation if in such a case the "inviter" should be vicariously liable for the hired domestic help who negligently poured hot sauce over the head of a guest but should not be equally liable for similar negligence on the part of the co-helper who was a neighbour and who had not been hired. In my view, in the latter case the person requested to assist in the service, but who was not hired for that purpose, is in the de facto service of the person who makes the request and for whom the duty is being performed." (per Walsh J).*

or anything which is reasonably incidental to his employment." (Ireland, 2012). However, if an employee is travelling from his home to his regular place of work, even in a company vehicle they are not acting in the course of their employment unless they MUST use the vehicle.

Section 15 of the Employment Equality Act 1998, which is entitled "Vicarious Liability, etc.," provides that "anything done by a person... in the course of his or her employment... shall be treated for the purposes of this Act... as done also by that person's employer, whether or not it was done with the employer's knowledge or approval." [48]

[47] *1 All ER 83*
http://www.margarethagan.com/wp-content/uploads/2013/03/law-donoghue-v-stevenson.png

Liability for Defective Products

Under the Liability for ***Defective Products Act 1991***, producers are liable for injury or damage caused by their defective products or defective components, irrespective of whether there was any negligence in the manufacturing process. Consumers have only to prove that there was an injury and that it was caused by a defect in the product. Proving that the producer was negligent is no longer necessary.[49] This tort is liability without fault based on public policy:

Strict liability

i.e. Product/manufacturer liability.
Manufacturers Strict Liability

Negligence-based product liability is based on a manufacturer's breach of the reasonable standard of care and failing to make a product safe. This is a no-fault principle, fault does not need to be proved, and that fact that the item was faulty and caused damage is sufficient. In other words, even if a person did not actually do something that caused injury, something they own, did.

Consumers are protected from unsafe products;

- Manufacturers should be liable to any user of the product;
- Manufacturers, sellers and distributors can bear the costs of injuries.

Liability for Defective Products Act 1991 (No. 28 of 1991)

This act gives effect to the provisions of Council Directive 85/374/EEC concerning liability for defective products. The main effect of the Act is to introduce into Irish law the principle of "strict" or "no fault" liability. This imposes liability on the producer, and in certain circumstances, the supplier of a defective product. The principle of strict liability is distinct from "fault" liability in which negligence on the part of the producer of the defective product must be proven. Strict liability is also distinct from "absolute" liability in that there are a number of defences available to the producer.

---

[49] *(Consumer Association of Ireland, 2010)*

Liability for Defective Products

Section 10 Defective Products Act 1991 prevents the producer from limiting or excluding his liability to injured consumers by using a term in a contract. ***Section 11 Defective Products Act 1991*** allows a plaintiff to bring a case in negligence if they are unable to bring a case within the strict liability regime laid down by the Act. The Act supplements existing civil law on product liability in tort and contract law. (Department of Jobs, Trade and Innovation, 2014). The Act was amended in 2000 to give effect to ***Council Directive 1999/34/EU*** which extended the definition of "*products*" in the Act to include primary agricultural products and game. The developments in products liability started with the thalidomide children, when these cases were originally brought, it was anxiety about tort's inability to deal with personal injury claims brought as a result of the use of the drug. The children claimants had no claim in contract; therefore, they had to rely on the tort of negligence. Where the plaintiff was required to prove a breach of the duty of care owed there was some difficulties which resulted in claimants losing their case in the UK, ***S v Distillers (Biochemicals) Ltd [1970]***[50]

Manufacturer must exercise "due care" in:

- Designing products;
- Manufacturing and Assembling Products;
- Inspecting and Testing Products; and
- Placing adequate warning labels

Defences to claims in product strict liability

- Product Misuse (Plaintiff does not know the product is dangerous for a particular use).
- Contributory/Comparative Negligence.
- Warning signs clearly marked.
- It is proved the defendant did not put the product into circulation.

[50] *1 WLR 114*

- Given the circumstances, it is probable that the defect did not exist at the time the product was put into circulation, or it came into being afterwards.
- The product was not manufactured for an economic purpose (e.g. sale, marketing) nor as part of the defendant's business.
- The defect arises out of compliance with EU law
- The state of scientific or technological knowledge when the product was circulated was not such as to allow the defect to be discovered.
- Where the product is a component, the defect lay in the design of the final product into which it was fitted (e.g. where a chandelier collapsed due to being dangerously overweighed with lights, the producer of an individual bulb would have a defence.)

Rylands V Fletcher

Rylands V Fletcher:

Strict Liability and Rylands v. Fletcher

The ***Rylands v. Fletcher [1868]*** case introduced into law a specific type of nuisance, one which is strict liability, the defendant may be liable even in the absence of any negligence on the defendant's part.

This imposition of liability has caused this case to be what can only amount of one of the most controversial and most used cases in the history of the study of Negligence and Tort.

However, its use is not as proficient as it once was. It can be stated that this case fell outside all the law of nuisance and negligence and trespass and thus creating its own precedent.

Affirmed by the H of L insofar as once the danger was created by the defendant, they must now bear the consequences of the risk they caused, or "fault based" principle in law.

Facts of the case

- John Rylands and Thomas Fletcher were neighbouring landowners, in 1860, Rylands instructed sub-contractors to build a reservoir on his land; this was for the purpose of supplying the Ainsworth Mill with water.
- Upon finding mine shafts which was loosely (debris and soil) connecting the two lands Rylands contractor made no effort to seal the shafts.
- When the reservoir was filled for the first time it burst and flooded Fletchers mine called the "colliery" causing £937.00 worth of damage.
- Fletcher pumped the mines out but after continuing use his pumps burst, causing the mine, to once again flood.
- The mine inspectors were instructed to attend the mines, whereby the connecting shafts were identified.

Rylands V Fletcher

Fletcher brought a case against Rylands in 1861 Exchequer Decision: Blackburn J. held that where a defendant brings something on his land for his benefit and knows it is likely to cause mischief if it escapes, he keeps it as his peril and is answerable for its escape.

Limited defences are available to the defendant HL Decision: Cairns L.J. modified the principle slightly, holding that the use of the thing must constitute a "non-natural" use of property to render the defendant liable. This can be explained as follows:

Exchequer: Blackburn J defined the rule as:

A person who, for his own purposes, brings onto land and keeps there anything likely to do mischief if it escapes, must do so at his peril, and, if he does not do so, he is prima facie answerable for all damage which is the natural consequence of its escape.

H of L: Cairns LJ

"On the other hand if the Defendants, not stopping at the natural use of their land, had desired to use it for any purpose which it may term a non-natural use, for the purpose of introducing into the land, that which in its natural condition was not in or upon it, for the purpose of introducing water either above or below ground in quantities and in a manner not the result of any work or operation on or under the land, - and if in consequence of their doing so, or in consequence of any imperfection in the mode of their doing so, the water came to escape and to pass off into the land of the Plaintiff, then it appears to me that that which the Defendants were doing they were doing at their own peril; and, if in the course of their doing it, the evil arose to which I have referred, the evil, namely, of the escape of the water and its passing away to the land of the Plaintiff and injuring the Plaintiff, then for the consequence of that, in my opinion, the Defendants would be liable."

*(**Explanation:** Rylands is a case which can cause confusion for students, one way to define and explain how this strict liability (no need to prove fault or negligence) is simply put, if you bring something onto*

"even your own land" and a reasonable person would not have that item or "thing" there, then you may be liable even if you take the most stringent of precaution, say for instance, you decide to buy a lion, you know this lion should not be in the reasonable persons garden, now say you build a cage, 20 x 20 and 3 m high, its extra strong metal, you ensure that there is alarms and cameras on the lions cage.... Now, even after all those precautions the lion escapes, and mauls a passer-by, even after all of your precautions, this would "technically" fall under Rylands. As the "thing" was unnatural (pet lion in a garden) and you are strictly liable for its actions no matter how it escaped or your precautions.)

Defences in Rylands

The principles laid out in Rylands v Fletcher [1868]

Requirements

1. Accumulation on the defendant's land Rylands v. Fletcher makes clear that: the principle applies only to things the defendant brings onto the property and not already ("naturally") there.

   - The accumulation must be intentional, but not deliberate, thus in ***Chu v. District of North Vancouver (1983):*** storage of food attracting rats was held to fall under the rule.

   - The thing must be accumulated for the defendant's own purposes: ***Northwestern Utilities v. London Guarantee & Accident Co. (1936):*** The defendant bringing things onto land for the purposes of provided public utilities (water, gas etc.) is for the public's benefit, such accumulations still fall under the rule, as the relevant companies are accumulating for their own purposes.

2. Place of Accumulation Ryland rule stated that the accumulation must be on the occupied land of the defendant; however the rule has been relaxed since, with ***Shell-Mex v. Belfast Corporation (1952)*** showing that the defendant can be a party who has permission or authority to use land, when they are in control of the dangerous item.

   - A thing likely to do mischief if it escapes. The thing need not be essentially hazardous; "anything likely to do mischief if it escapes". The escape itself does not have to be foreseeable.

3. Escape The thing must have escaped from the defendant's land. Escape is limited to unintentional escape, as an intentional escape gives rise to other torts, e.g. trespass. N.B, the act leading to the escape can be intentional, but the escape must be unintentional. This requirement is satisfied if either the accumulated item or its dangerous effects escape: ***Rylands v. Fletcher (1868)*** itself is an example of the accumulated item

escaping; ***Miles v. Forest Rock Granite (1918)*** is an example of the effects escaping, namely rocks which damaged property after blasting operations, where explosives were held to the be accumulated item.

4. Non-natural use of land

Cairns L.J. in Rylands v Fletcher, held the use of gathering water for a mill's reservoir to be non-natural, but stated that water seeping to the plaintiff's coal mines by means of the milling process would have been natural. Moulton L.J. in Rickards v. Lothian (1913) – there must be "some special use bringing with it increase risk to others". Therefore, water or gas in normal domestic quantities would be natural; however, vast amounts for commercial purposes would be non-natural.

5. The damage must not be too remote Liability in Rylands v. Fletcher is subject to the rules on remoteness of damage. ***Cambridge Water v. Eastern Counties Leather (1994)*** introduced an ordinary negligence test into this element of the tort: the plaintiff must show that the danger of the damage was reasonably foreseeable to the defendant (i.e. foreseeability of the item's existence, it's possible escape and the possible harm).

Would a Plaintiff make a claim in negligence or under the Rylands v. Fletcher rule?

Identifying the distinction to the rule in Rylands v. Fletcher and the rule of negligence is very difficult, it can be said that any claimant who could succeed in Ryland v. Fletcher may succeed in negligence. ***Burnie Port Authority v. General Jones (1994)***:

Defences in Rylands

Defences:

Below are the main defences for Rylands v. Fletcher:

1. act of a stranger
2. volenti non fit injura
3. statutory authority
4. default of the claimant
5. act of God

Act of a Stranger

If the escape was caused by a stranger (a third party over whom the defendant had no control), this will be a defence. In ***Rickards v Lothian (1913)***, the tap that flooded the claimant's premises was turned on by a stranger, and the claim failed.

Volenti non fit injura (consent/willingly)

It is a defence if the claimant consented to the defendant bringing the dangerous thing onto his or her land. This defence will be particularly strong if the thing on the defendant's land benefits the claimant. A common benefit e.g. neighbours benefit from water storage on the defendant's land, means that a claim would fail if there were an escape.

Statutory Authority

An Act of the Oireachtas may authorise a dangerous activity, and therefore there can be no claim under Rylands v Fletcher. Some statutes specify if the rule applies and others do not, so it is up to the judge to decide. In ***Green v Chelsea Waterworks Co. (1894)***, the waterworks company was under a duty authorised by Parliament to provide water.

This meant that a claim for damage caused by a leak from the pipe failed, as it was foreseeable that bursts could occur.

Defences in Rylands

Default of the claimant

If the escape and damage are caused completely by the default of the claimant, the defendant will not be liable. If the claimant is partly responsible, the normal rules of contributory negligence apply, and the compensation will be reduced accordingly.

Act of God

Extreme weather conditions may afford a defence. However, the courts are reluctant to allow this defence unless the weather conditions are exceptional. In ***Nichols v Marsland (1876***), there was a successful use of this defence when the claimant's land was flooded after extremely heavy rainfall caused the defendant's ornamental lakes to flood Damage and Causation Damage is an essential element, unless the plaintiff seeks a quia timet injunction to prevent impending harm.

Case law makes clear that:

a) there must be physical damage to land;

b) and flowing from this a consequential economic loss;

c) there must be damage to chattels; and

d) personal injury are all recoverable claims.

The law is less clear on non-owner/occupiers of the neighbouring land, but it can amount to a claim in nuisance.

Quia Timet ("because he fears") injunction prevent anticipated infringement of a legal right however, the plaintiff must be able to establish a sufficiently strong case of threatened loss. ***AGV Rathmines and Pembroke Joint Hospital Board*** states: that the Plaintiff must have a well-grounded apprehension of injury, *"almost amounting to a moral certainty"*.

Statute of Limitations Act 1957 – Tort

Statute of limitations **Act 1957**

(TORT) 6 years for conversion, detinue trespass, nuisance etc.

HOWEVER, **Personal Injury** is two years

Defamation = one year – statute of limitations act 1957.

Case Summaries and Rulings in Tort

Below are cases in Tort – Please research each one and define the case summary and the ruling, I have already put the heading under which each case falls, I have already filled out the first one for you.

List of cases in tort

Vicarious Liability:

Moynihan v Moynihan:

Summary = A Granddaughter was burnt by tea which was poured by her aunt on her grandmothers instructions, neither the child or the aunt lived at the house – Defence argued that the aunt did not live there nor was it her house so the instructions of the grandmother were not vicariously liable

Ruling = HELD: the court found the homeowner is liable to the actions of a visitor once they give them instructions

Research and fill out the following:
McKenna V Best Travel
Summary________________________________
Ruling =

Trespass to the Person:
Scott v Shephard:
Summary________________________________
Ruling =

Battery:
Cole v Turner:
R v Cotesworth:
Summary________________________________
Ruling =

Assault:
Stephens v Myers:
R v Ireland:
Summary________________________________

Ruling =

False Imprisonment:
Brid v Jones:
Hearing v Boyle:
Summary________________________________
Ruling =

Defences:
Self Defence:
Cregan v O'Sullivan:
Summary________________________________
Ruling =

Consent:
Summary________________________________
Ruling =

Necessity:
Lawful Authority:
Summary________________________________
Ruling =

Trespass to Goods:
Farrell v Minister for Agri & Food:
Summary________________________________
Ruling =

Detinue:
Poole v Burns:
Summary________________________________
Ruling =

Conversion:
Hollins v Fowler:
Summary________________________________
Ruling =

Trespass to Land:
O'Brien v McNamee:

Whelan v Madigan:
Summary________________________________
Ruling =

Remedies:
Re-entry, Ejectment, Mesne Profits and Damages. Injunctions in relation to a continuing trespass.
Summary________________________________
Ruling =

Defences:
Consent, Lawful Authority.
Summary________________________________
Ruling =

Necessity:
Cope v Sharpe:
Summary________________________________
Ruling =

Strict Liability
Rylands v Fletcher:
Summary________________________________
Ruling =

Nuisance:
Connolly v South of Ireland Asphalt Co:
Summary________________________________
Ruling =

Defence to nuisance
Sturges v Brideman:
Summary________________________________
Ruling =

Consent:
Thomas v Lewis:
Summary________________________________
Ruling =

Case Summaries and Rulings in Tort

Public Nuisance:
Mullar v Foster:
Cunningham v McGrath Brothers:
Summary________________________________
Ruling =

Passing Off:
Polycell Products Ltd v O'Carroll & Ors:
McCambridge ltd v Joseph Brennan Bakeries: 2012: SCt:
Summary________________________________
Ruling =

Goodwill?
An Post v Irish Permanent:
DSG Retail v PC World:
Summary________________________________
Ruling =

Misrepresentation/Confusion?
Jameson v Irish Distillers:
Jiff lemon case:
Summary________________________________
Ruling =

Damage:
Falcon Travel v Owners Abroad Group:
Summary________________________________
Ruling =

Negligence: Define ________________
Duty of Care
Donoghue Stephenson
Kirby v Burke & Holloway
Hedley Byrne v Heller
Anns v Merton London Borough Council
Caparo Industries v Dickman
Glencar v Mayo Co Co
Summary________________________________
Ruling =

Standard of care:
Haley v London Electricity Board:
Summary______________________________
Ruling =

Causation:
Kenny v O'Rourke:
Summary______________________________
Ruling =

MATERIAL CONTRIBUTION TEST:
McGhee v National Coal Board:
Quinn v Midwestern Health Board:
Skull rule and remoteness of damage.
Breslin & Corcoran & MIBI:
Summary______________________________
Ruling =

Remoteness of Damage:
Re Polemis:
Condon v CIS:
Summary______________________________
Ruling =

Egg Shell Skull Rule:
Smith v Leech Brain & Co Ltd:
Summary______________________________
Ruling =

Res Ipsa Loquitor:
Scott v London St Katherine Docks Co:
Summary______________________________
Ruling =
Pure Economic Loss:
Hedley Byrne v Heller:
Ward v McMaster:
Summary______________________________
Ruling =

Professional Negligence:

Dunne v The National Maternity Hospital:
Summary________________________________

Ruling =
Solicitors' Negligence:
Roche v Peilow:
Summary________________________________

Ruling =
Defamation:
Quigley v Creation:
Speight V Gosnay
Summary________________________________
Ruling =

Defamation
Berry v Irish Times:
Reynolds v Malocco:
Reynolds v Times Newspapers:
Talbot v Hermitage Golf club:
Summary________________________________
Ruling =

Occupiers Liability:
Power v Governor of Cork Prison:
Summary________________________________
Ruling =

Product Liability:
O'Byrne v Gloucester & Ors:
Summary________________________________
Ruling =
Employer's Liability:
Connolly v Dundalk UDC & Mahon & Philips:
Summary________________________________
Ruling =
Standard of Care:
Harris v Bright Asphalt:
Summary________________________________
Ruling =

Limitation of Actions:

Statute of Limitations – 6 years for tort (assault, battery, trespass, etc) from date on which cause of action accrued- BUT now 2 years for personal injury

Defamation - 1 year

Devlin v Roche:

Summary________________________________

Ruling =

Undiscovered property damage? (statute of limitations)

O'Donnell v Kilsaran Concrete Ltd:

Summary________________________________

Ruling

=

Law of Tort -- Multiple Choice Questions

1. What is the standard of care applied to professionals with a special skill or expertise?
   a) That of the reasonable person with the same skill or expertise
   b) That of the reasonable person in that profession
   c) That of the reasonably qualified person
   d) That of the reasonable person with the same level of experience or skill in that profession.

2. What does a claimant need to show to establish liability in a negligence claim?
   1. There was a duty of care
   2. That the duty was not breached
   3. The breach caused damage
   4. The damage was foreseeable
      a) 1, 2 and 4 only
      b) 1, 3 and 4 only
      c) 2 and 3 only
      d) All of the above

3. What does the "*eggshell skull*" rule mean?
   a) That defendant is not liable where the plaintiff had a pre-existing injury
   b) That defendants must take their victims as they find them
   c) The defendant is liable for injuries which would be foreseen by a reasonable person
   d) None of the above

4. Which of the following may give rise to vicarious liability?
   1. Vehicle owners and their permitted drivers.
   2. Employer and employee.
   3. Teachers and pupils in their care during school hours.
      a) 1 and 2 only
      b) 1 and 3 only
      c) 2 and 3 only
      d) 1, 2 and 3 only

5. Which case ruled that where a person who is visiting the house, acts on the instruction of the owner of the property, the owner is liable for their acts?
   a) Re Polomis
   b) Hadley v Baxendale
   c) Speight V Gosnay
   d) Moynihan v Moynihan

6. Define the meaning of the defence *volenti non fit injuria*?
   a) There is no liability on the defendant where the plaintiff has voluntary assumed the risk
   b) The person who causes the injury must be held liable
   c) The compensation must fit the damages
   d) None of the above

7. Where a defendant can prove contributory negligence against the plaintiff, they are proving
   a) The plaintiff did not contribute to their own injuries
   b) The defendant contributed to the plaintiff's injuries
   c) The plaintiff contributed to their own injuries
   d) None of the above

8. Sarah is learning to drive; she is negligent and mounts the kerb, injuring her driving instructor, what is Sarah's duty of care in this case
   a) There is a driver to driver duty of care owed
   b) The duty owed is that of a reasonable learner driver
   c) The duty of care is that owed by a learner driver
   d) All of the Above

9. Interference with another's enjoyment of life or property is known as:
   a) Trespass
   b) Nuisance
   c) Defamation
   d) None of the above

10. A wrongful act that injures another's reputation with false statements is known as:
   a) Trespass

b) Nuisance
c) Defamation
d) None of the above

11. The failure to exercise the degree of care that a reasonable person would exercise those results in the proximate cause of actual harm to an innocent person is known as:
a) Strict Liability
b) Nuisance
c) Defamation
d) Negligence

12. The tort that results when one person deliberately frightens another person into the reasonable belief that he or she is about to be injured is known as:
a) Assault
b) Battery
c) Assault and Battery
d) Grievous bodily harm

13. Manufacturers product Strict Liability requires
a) Fault
b) No fault
c) Damage
d) None of the above

14. The rule in ***Mc Kenna V Best travel*** stated that
a) There were liable as they had brought the defendant to a dangerous territory
b) They were not liable as they had got the plaintiff to sign a disclaimer before leaving
c) There were not guilty as they had no specialised knowledge of the risks
d) They were not guilty as the plaintiff had voluntarily went to the danger

15. The requirement that, the damage need not be foreseeable was a ruling in the case of:
a) Hadley v Baxendale
b) Carlill v Carbolic Smokeball

c) Re Polomis
d) Quigley v Creation

16. The court ruling in ***Speight v Gosnay*** stated that:
   a) Where a statement lowers the applicant in the eyes of a community the defendant is liable in defamation
   b) The applicant can bring a case in defamation if they receive a defamatory letter from an individual; they are the only ones to read it.
   c) The defendant is liable if the plaintiff reads the defamatory statement and is upset
   d) The defendant is liable if another person republishes the defamatory statement even if it is withdrawn by the original poster

17. Liquidated damages are
   a) Quantifiable
   b) Unquantifiable
   c) Unknown
   d) None of the above

18. ***Grant v Australian Knitting Mills*** involved which Tort:
   a) Negligence
   b) Nuisance
   c) Defamation
   d) Assault

19. The Irish precedent case in defining the Duty of Care owed is:
   a) Donoghue v Stevenson
   b) Carlill v Carbolic Smokeball
   c) Glencar v Mayo Co Co
   d) Caparo Industries v Dickman Plc

20. Remoteness of damages can be defined as:
   a) Proximity of the parties
   b) Duty of care owed
   c) Reasonable Foreseeability
   d) Standard of Care

21. Which of the following is a defence in Nuisance

a) It is a quarry, there will be noise
b) The levels of noise are acceptable
c) Prescription
d) All of the above

22. Strict liability occurs when;
a) There is no requirement to find fault
b) Fault must be established
c) Fault is established one the duty of care is established
d) The parties agree there is fault

23. The tort of passing off occurs when
a) A seller sells his own goods on his own market stalls
b) A seller sells goods and leads buyers to believe they are the goods of a competitor
c) A buyer believes the goods on sale are branded goods and buys them
d) A seller tells the buyer the goods look like those of a competitor, but they are not

24. Interference with another's enjoyment of life or property is known as
a) Defamation
a) Tort
b) Trespass to the Person
c) Nuisance

25. The tort of Conversion is defined as;
a) a person lending a neighbor their lawnmower
b) taking another person property and using for personal gain
c) giving property back to the owner when they ask for it
d) none of the above

26. The tort that results when one person deliberately frightens another person into the reasonable belief that he or she is about to be injured is known as:
a) conversion
b) tort
c) assault
d) battery

27. Failure to return goods to the owner when requested is called;
    a) conversion
    b) nuisance
    c) trespass to the person
    d) detinue

28. Prescription is a defence to
    a) nuisance
    b) trespass to land
    c) nuisance
    d) defamation

29. Statutory Authority gets its power from
    a) legislation
    b) common law
    c) prescription
    d) case law

30. ***Res Ipsa Loquitur*** means.
    a) the solicitor speaks with the prosecution
    b) the thing speaks for itself
    c) the defendant speaks for themselves
    d) the barrister speaks for the defendant

31. Liability for dangerous or "unnatural things" stems from the case of;
    a) Donoghue v Stevenson
    b) Hadley v Baxendale
    c) Quigley v Creaton
    d) Rylands v Fletcher

32. Despite the defendant not having done anything wrong, they may still be held liable in tort under:
    a) negligence
    b) strict liability
    c) defamation
    d) trespass

33. An employer's liability for the actions of their employee, who is acting outside the scope of their employment, or outside their working time, has;
a) vicarious liability
b) no liability
c) employer's liability
d) employees' rights at work

34. Slander is defined as;
a) the spoken word
b) the written word
c) words found online
d) none of the above

35. Libel is defined as;
a) the spoken word
b) the written word
c) words found online
d) none of the above

36. In defamation, opinions are generally
a) actionable
b) nonactionable
c) libellous
d) slanderous

37. In defamation, republication is actionable as per;
a) Quigley v Creation
b) Speight v Gosney
c) Donoghue v Stevenson
d) Hadley v Baxendale

38. To be defamatory, a statement must,
a) be told to the defendant
b) be told to the general public
c) be communicated to a third party
d) be thought by the defendant

39. Which case laid down the precedent in determining the duty of care?

a) Donoghue v Stevenson
b) Fischer v bell
c) Caparo Industries v Dickman Plc.
d) Partridge v Crittenden

40. Mitigation of losses means;
a) The defendant must take reasonable care to ensure they do not damage the plaintiff's goods
b) The plaintiff must take reasonable steps to reduce their own losses
c) The plaintiff must take every step possible to reduce their own losses
d) The defendant must take reasonable steps to reduce their plaintiff's losses

41. Which of the following cases resulted in the court finding that cost of avoiding the risk outweighed the risk and found that the defendant was not negligent.
a) The Wagon Mound 2
b) Latimer v AEC
c) Donoghue v Stevenson
d) Caparo Industries v Dickman Plc.

42. The case of ***McGhee v National Coal Board*** is relevant to
a) The "but for" test
b) Causation
c) Remoteness of damage
d) Material contribution test

43. Which of the following is NOT a type of damages
a) Nominal damages
b) Exemplary damages
c) Aggravated damages
d) Contemporary damages

44. Which case was the claimant found to have contributed to their injuries
a) Livox Quarries v Boyce
b) Jones v Boyce
c) Jones v Livox Quarries

d) Smith v Jones

45. Contributory negligence occurs when:
a) The claimant was hurt because of the actions of the defendant
b) The claimant was a reasonable person who was hurt due to another's actions
c) The claimant was wholly or partly to blame for their own injuries
d) The claimant was an innocent victim in an accident

46. How does the courts best determine if an employer is vicariously liable for the actions of staff?
a) Control test
b) The reasonable man tests
c) Proximity test
d) Fair just and reasonable

47. What is the closest description of the *reasonable man*
a) He is very cautious
b) He is very safety conscious
c) He was low intelligence
d) He is neither very cautious nor does he take excessive risks

48. Vicariously liable' means
a) A person is responsible for another's actions
b) A person is not responsible for another's actions
c) A person is responsible for their own actions
d) None of The Above

49. What is the purpose of determining if a duty of care exists
a) To ensure that all parties are treated fairly
b) To determine who is liable for the damage
c) It ensures that the right person is sued
d) To determine if the wrongdoer was actually careless

50. Why did Mrs. Donoghue bring an action in tort and not in contract?
a) She was not a party to the contract and therefore the only avenue was tort

b) She had a contract which was frustrated so had to bring an action in tort
c) She had the ginger beer drank before she seen the snail, so contract was discharged
d) She bought the ginger beer with her friends' money, so she had no contract

Law of Tort MCQ ANSWERS

1. What is the standard of care applied to professionals with a special skill or expertise?
   a) That of the reasonable person with the same skill or expertise
   b) That of the reasonable person in that profession
   c) That of the reasonably qualified person
   d) That of the reasonable person with the same level of experience or skill in that profession.

2. What does a claimant need to show to establish liability in a negligence claim?
   1. There was a duty of care
   2. That the duty was not breached
   3. The breach caused damage
   4. The damage was foreseeable
      a. 1, 2 and 4 only
      b. 1, 3 and 4 only
      c. 2 and 3 only
      d. All of the above

3. What does the "*eggshell skull*" rule mean?
   a) That defendant is not liable where the plaintiff had a pre-existing injury
   b) That defendants must take their victims as they find them
   c) The defendant is liable for injuries which would be foreseen by a reasonable person
   d) None of the above

4. Which of the following may give rise to vicarious liability?
   1. Vehicle owners and their permitted drivers.
   2. Employer and employee.
   3. Teachers and pupils in their care during school hours.
   a. 1 and 2 only
   b. 1 and 3 only
   c. 2 and 3 only
   d. 1, 2 and 3 only

5. Which case ruled that where a person who is visiting a house, acts on the instruction of the owner of the property, the owner is liable for their acts?
   a) Re Polomis

b) Hadley v Baxendale
c) Speight V Gosnay
d) Moynihan v Moynihan

6. Define the meaning of the defence *volenti non fit injuria*?
a) There is no liability on the defendant where the plaintiff has voluntary assumed the risk
b) The person who causes the injury must be held liable
c) The compensation must fit the damages
d) None of the above

7. Where a defendant can prove contributory negligence against the plaintiff, they are proving
a) The plaintiff did not contribute to their own injuries
b) The defendant contributed to the plaintiffs injuries
c) The plaintiff contributed to their own injuries
d) None of the above

8. Sarah is learning to drive; she is negligent and mounts the kerb, injuring her driving instructor, what is Sarah's duty of care in this case
a) There is a driver to driver duty of care owed
b) The duty owed is that of a reasonable learner driver
c) The duty of care is that owed by a learner driver
d) All of the Above

9. Interference with another's enjoyment of life or property is known as:
a) Trespass
b) Nuisance
c) Defamation
d) None of the above

10. A wrongful act that injures another's reputation with false statements is known as:
a) Trespass
b) Nuisance
c) Defamation
d) None of the above

Law of Tort MCQ ANSWERS

11. The failure to exercise the degree of care that a reasonable person would exercise those results in the proximate cause of actual harm to an innocent person is known as:

a) Strict Liability
b) Nuisance
c) Defamation
d) Negligence

12. The tort that results when one person deliberately frightens another person into the reasonable belief that he or she is about to be injured is known as:

a) Assault
b) Battery
c) Assault and Battery
d) Grievous bodily harm

13. Manufacturers product Strict Liability requires

a) Fault
b) No fault
c) Damage
d) None of the above

14. The rule in ***<u>Mc Kenna V Best travel</u>*** stated that

a) There were liable as they had brought the defendant to a dangerous territory
b) They were not liable as they had got the plaintiff to sign a disclaimer before leaving
c) There were not guilty as they had no specialised knowledge of the risks
d) They were not guilty as the plaintiff had voluntarily went to the danger

15. The requirement that, the damage need not be foreseeable was a ruling in the case of:

a) Hadley v Baxendale
b) Carlill v Carbolic smokeball
c) Re Polomis
d) Quigley v Creation

Law of Tort MCQ ANSWERS

16. The court ruling in ***Speight v Gosnay*** stated that:
    a) Where a statement lowers the applicant in the eyes of a community the defendant is liable in defamation
    b) The applicant can bring a case in defamation if they receive a defamatory letter from an individual; they are the only ones to read it.
    c) The defendant is liable if the plaintiff reads the defamatory statement and is upset
    d) The defendant is liable if another person republishes the defamatory statement even if it is withdrawn by the original poster

17. Liquidated damages are
    a) Quantifiable
    b) Unquantifiable
    c) Unknown
    d) None of the above

18. ***Grant v Australian Knitting Mills*** involved which Tort:
    a) Negligence
    b) Nuisance
    c) Defamation
    d) Assault

19. The Irish precedent case in defining the Duty of Care owed is:
    a) Donoghue v Stevenson
    b) Carlill v Carbolic Smokeball
    c) Glencar v Mayo Co Co
    d) Caparo Industries v Dickman Plc.

20. Remoteness of damages can be defined as:
    a) Proximity of the parties
    b) Duty of care owed
    c) Reasonable Foreseeability
    d) Standard of Care

21. Which of the following is a defence in Nuisance
    a) It is a quarry, there will be noise
    b) The levels of noise are acceptable

c) **Prescription**
d) All of the above

22. Strict liability occurs when;
a) There is no requirement to find fault
b) Fault must be established
c) Fault is established one the duty of care is established
d) The parties agree there is fault

23. The tort of passing off occurs when
a) A seller sells his own goods on his own market stalls
b) A seller sells goods and leads buyers to believe they are the goods of a competitor
c) A buyer believes the goods on sale are branded goods and buys them
d) A seller tells the buyer the goods look like those of a competitor but they are not

24. Interference with another's enjoyment of life or property is known as
a) Defamation
b) Tort
c) Trespass to the Person
d) Nuisance

25. The tort of Conversion is defined as;
a) a person lending a neighbour their lawnmower
b) taking another person property and using for personal gain
c) giving property back to the owner when they ask for it
d) none of the above

26. The tort that results when one person deliberately frightens another person into the reasonable belief that he or she is about to be injured is known as:
a) conversion
b) tort
c) assault
d) battery

Law of Tort MCQ ANSWERS

27. Failure to return goods to the owner when requested is called;
    a) conversion
    b) nuisance
    c) trespass to the person
    d) detinue

28. Prescription is a defence to
a) nuisance
b) trespass to land
c) nuisance
d) defamation

29. Statutory Authority gets its power from
a) legislation
b) common law
c) prescription
d) case law

30. ***Res Ipsa Loquitur*** means.
a) the solicitor speaks with the prosecution
b) the thing speaks for itself
c) the defendant speaks for themself
d) the barrister speaks for the defendant

31. Liability for dangerous or "unnatural things" stems from the case of;
a) Donoghue v Stevenson
b) Hadley v Baxendale
c) Quigley v Creation
d) Rylands v Fletcher

32. Despite the defendant not having done anything wrong, they may still be held liable in tort under:
a) negligence
b) strict liability
c) defamation
d) trespass

Law of Tort MCQ ANSWERS

33. An employer's liability for the actions of their employee, who is acting outside the scope of their employment, or outside their working time, has;
a) vicarious liability
b) no liability
c) employers liability
d) employees' rights at work

34. Slander is defined as;
a) the spoken word
b) the written word
c) words found online
d) none of the above
35. Libel is defined as;
a) the spoken word
b) the written word
c) words found online
d) none of the above

36. In defamation, opinions are *generally*
a) actionable
b) non actionable
c) libellous
d) slanderous

37. In defamation, republication is actionable as per;
a) Quigley v Creation
b) Speight v Gosney
c) Donoghue v Stevenson
d) Hadley v Baxendale

38. To be defamatory, a statement must,
a) be told to the defendant
b) be told to the general public
c) be communicated to a third party
d) be thought by the defendant

39. Which case laid down the precedent in determining the duty of care?
a) Donoghue v Stevenson

b) Fischer v bell
c) Caparo Industries v Dickman Plc.
d) Partridge v Crittenden

40. Mitigation of losses means;
a) The defendant must take reasonable care to ensure they do not damage the plaintiff's goods
b) The plaintiff must take reasonable steps to reduce their own losses
c) The plaintiff must take every step possible to reduce their own losses
d) The defendant must take reasonable steps to reduce their plaintiff's losses

41. Which of the following cases resulted in the court finding that cost of avoiding the risk outweighed the risk and found that the defendant was not negligent.
a) The Wagon Mound 2
b) Latimer v AEC
c) Donoghue v Stevenson
d) Caparo Industries v Dickman Plc.

42. The case of ***McGhee v National Coal Board*** is relevant to
a) The "but for" test
b) Causation
c) Remoteness of damage
d) Material contribution test

43. Which of the following is NOT a type of damages
a) Nominal damages
b) Exemplary damages
c) Aggravated damages
d) Contemporary damages

44. Which case was the claimant found to have contributed to their injuries
a) Livox Quarries v Boyce
b) Jones v Boyce
c) Jones v Livox Quarries
d) Smith v Jones

Law of Tort MCQ ANSWERS

45. Contributory negligence occurs when:

a) The plaintiff was hurt because of the actions of the defendant
b) The plaintiff was a reasonable person who was hurt due to another's actions
c) The plaintiff was wholly or partly to blame for their own injuries
d) The plaintiff was an innocent victim in an accident

46. How does the courts best determine if an employer is vicariously liable for the actions of staff?

a) Is the employee carrying out an authorised act
b) The reasonable man test
c) Proximity test
d) Fair just and reasonable

47. What is the closest description of the *reasonable man*

a) He is very cautious
b) He is very safety conscious
c) He was low intelligence
d) He is neither very cautious nor does he take excessive risks

48. Vicariously liable' means

e) A person is responsible for another's actions
f) A person is not responsible for another's actions
g) A person is responsible for their own actions
h) None Of The Above

49. What is the purpose of determining if a duty of care exists

a) To ensure that all parties are treated fairly
b) To determine who is liable for the damage
c) It ensure that the right person is sued
d) To determine if the wrongdoer was actually careless

50. Why did Mrs Donoghue bring an action in tort and not in contract?

a) She was not a party to the contract and therefore the only avenue was tort
b) She had a contract which was frustrated so had to bring an action in tort

c) She had the ginger beer drank before she seen the snail so contract was discharged
d) She bought the ginger beer with her friends money so she had no contract

Conclusion

The law of Tort concerns civil wrongs, however, from your study above you can see that not every civil wrong, is a tort. A Tort is a civil wrong which can be compensated for, by a case for damages and which is a different branch of law, to say, than a mere breach of contract or breach of trust.

In a compensation case for example, when a plaintiff looks for damages in tort, the Court awards pecuniary compensation to the plaintiff for the injury or damage caused to him by the wrongful act of the defendant. Tort law is dynamic and ever-changing; this is because of its interdependence on social structures and an ever changing judiciary. Precedent continues to play an active part in court decision and most due to the lack of specific legislation dealing with many cases in hand, obviously there cannot be legislation for every single what if, but the law of tort has done an amazing job so far.

Lighter Side of the Law

The lighter side of the law

Not everything about the law needs to be staunch and boring, in fact the law is exciting, dynamic and interesting, its can however be difficult sometimes to find humour or fun when you are trying to get to grips with the doctrines, rules and principles.

I will finish off this book on a lighter note, a selection of Irish laws and of course International ones too, so that you can see the lighter side of the law before you close the book. Enjoy and have a giggle, or even awe (maybe)

Ireland has its fair share of strange and (by modern standards) weird laws.

Plain Weird Laws in Ireland

1. It is illegal to perform witchcraft in Ireland: Any person who shall pretend or exercise to use any type of witchcraft, sorcery, enchantment, or pretend knowledge in any occult or craft or science shall for any such offense suffer imprisonment at the time of one whole year and also shall be obliged to obscursion for his/her good behaviour.

2: It is illegal for a student to walk through Trinity College without a sword.

3: In Trinity college students can demand a glass of brandy at any time during an exam, provided they are wearing their sword and hand it up.

4. It is illegal to be drunk in a pub, (it is illegal for landlords to continue to serve alcohol to an intoxicated person)

5. It is illegal to smoke tobacco on Grafton Street.

6. If a Leprechaun calls at your door you must, by law, give him a share of your dinner.

7. Holders of the freedom of Dublin have the right to pasture sheep on common ground within the city boundaries. (Remember Bono and the sheep grazing in Dublin?). However, some say that by doing so they accidentally broke the law at the same time as you are only allowed to graze your own sheep, not borrowed ones.

8. *The Tippling Act 1735* prohibits a publican from pursuing a customer for money owed for any drink given on credit. (How many slates are illegally followed?)

9. (Any aspiring Sheldon's beware). It is illegal to conduct nuclear tests in the city. This law from 2006 clearly states that: "A person who carries out, or causes the carrying out of, a nuclear explosion in the State shall be guilty of an offense."

10. Crossing a railway track on a bicycle is illegal whereas you can drive across it legally. You are still supposed to dismount and walk your bike across at a level crossing.

And Whacky Laws

1. You can shoot someone and kill them from the top of the campinile (bell tower) in Trinity College, on a particular day of the year and not be charged with murder. However, it is impossible to find out what day of the year it is....

2. Law: It is illegal to operate a flashing amber beacon on an agricultural tractor (and many other vehicles).

Repealed Laws

3. Henry VIII declared that: a pilot of a ship who runs aground in Dublin Bay will be blinded as punishment for their incompetence.

4. The penalty for suicide was death by hanging. [51])

---

[51] *(http://www.staycity.com/category-dublin/15-unbelievable-laws-in-dublin-you-might-have-to-adhere-to-while-in-the-city/*

Lighter Side of the Law

Some newspaper excepts from Irish cases

Humour in court can heal drugs pain - Anne-Marie Walsh

May 5 2006 12:11 AM

COMEDIAN Des Bishop dispensed words of wisdom from the judge's bench yesterday as two men graduated with honours in the difficult subject of ditching drugs.

The Corkman kept the court in stitches as he praised the efforts made by the latest Drugs Treatment Court success stories - a 23-year-old with a cocaine addiction and a 32-year-old heroin addict who have come through two of the most gruelling years of their lives.

Both men, who did not want to be named, are part of a pioneering system of drugs rehab that rewards participants by dropping charges against them as they progress.

As they go through months of 'cold turkey' that includes regular urine tests, schooling and counselling, they gradually whittle down their charges to zero.

The outcome is the unfamiliar sight of a happy courtroom where the perpetrators of crime are applauded as they are rewarded by a judge.

Judge Bridget Reilly also promised a 'surprise' in the shape of comedian Des Bishop. The room was in stitches when he joked "I could get €5 for that".[52]

---

[52] *http://www.independent.ie/irish-news/humour-in-court-can-heal-drugs-pain-26383053.html*

Lighter Side of the Law

I Got an Apology from the Barrister

Calmness is over and it's back to mayhem. I was actually in the High Court in Dublin last week as a witness in a case where basically a publican is trying to get a pub license. While one of the owners was in the witness box, the state's senior council said that the Cully and Sully pies were just fast food and the same as Cuisine De France - which I took serious exception to. I was then called into the witness box and asked to outline who our customers were so I told the Judge that our customers included Cleary's Tearooms restaurant, Bank Of Ireland and that actually we are about to start supplying the Four Courts at the request of some high court judges!!!!! I then turned around to the States Barrister and told her that "indeed we were not Cuisine De France". To which the entire court erupted in laughter and I got an apology from the barrister.

Brilliant. I then legged it out of the box!!!!!!![53]

And...

Longford District Court Sitting – 2016 (my own)

Defendant: (an elderly man), was called to the stand, charged with speeding; the defendant slowly makes his way to the witness box.........

Judge; you are charged; on x day 2016, you were found to be spee........ Ring...Ring...... defendant's mobile phone rings;

Defendant: judge, can I take this.... Judge; feel free ... defendant; I can't talk right now, I'm in court, (other party .....!) no I'm talking to the judge .....(Courtroom erupts in laughter)

---

[53] *http://www.cullyandsully.com/content/i-got-apology-barrister[last accessed 2nd Mary 2017]*

Lighter Side of the Law

Weird Laws in the United Kingdom

1. Since 1313, MPs are not allowed to don armour in Parliament.

2. No cows may be driven down the roadway between 10 AM and 7 PM unless there is prior approval from the Commissioner of Police.

3. All land must be left to the eldest son. (not just the UK.... Huh)

4. Excluding Sundays, it is perfectly legal to shoot a Scotsman with a bow and arrow.

5. A bed may not be hung out of a window.

6. *It is legal for a male to urinate in public, as long it is on the rear wheel of his motor vehicle and his right hand is on the vehicle.*

7. A license is required to keep a lunatic.

8. It is illegal for a lady to eat chocolates on a public conveyance.

9. Committing suicide is classified as a capital crime.

10. With the exception of carrots, most goods may not be sold on Sunday.

11. It is illegal to shoot a Welshman with a crossbow on Thursdays.

12. In Liverpool, it is illegal for a woman to be topless except as a clerk in a tropical fish store.

13. Any person found breaking a boiled egg at the sharp end will be sentenced to 24 hours in the village stocks (enacted by Edward VI).

Lighter Side of the Law

And of Course, Plain Crazy from the USA

1. Bear wrestling matches are prohibited.

2. Incestuous marriages are legal. (In Alabama)

3. You may not have an ice cream cone in your back pocket at any time.

4. It is considered an offense to open an umbrella on a street, for fear of spooking horses.

5. Women are able to retain all property they owned prior to marriage in the case of divorce. However, this provision does not apply to men. (Interesting, and quite unfair)

6. It is illegal to sell peanuts in Lee County after sundown on Wednesday.

7. It is illegal for a driver to be blindfolded while operating a vehicle.

8. It is illegal to wear a fake moustache that causes laughter in church.

9. Putting salt on a railroad track may be punishable by death.

10. Men who deflower virgins, regardless of age or marital status, may face up to five years in jail.

Glossary of Terms

Glossary of Terms

Acceptance: An unqualified agreement to the terms of the offer.

Administrator: A person appointed by the court to carry out an administration.

Agent: A person authorised to act for another (the principal) and bring that other into legal relations with a third party.

Annual general meeting (AGM) : Every company (except ltd) is required to hold a meeting of each its members each (calendar) year, at intervals of not more than 15 months, at which it is usual, but not obligatory to transact the 'ordinary business' of the company. Such business may include consideration of the accounts, declaration of a dividend and appointment of auditors.

Anticipatory breach: Renunciation by party to a contract of his contractual obligations before the date for performance.

Arbitration: A means of settling a dispute outside the courts.

Articles of association: Rules governing the internal conduct of a company's affairs, such as appointment, powers and proceedings of directors, alteration of capital structure, dividends and so on.

Auditor: A person appointed by the company in general meeting to report whether the accounts reflect a true and fair view of the company's affairs.

Business name: A name used by a company other than the registered one.

Capacity: The ability or power of a person to enter into legal relationships or carry out legal acts.

Care, duty of: The care owed by one person to another which, if broken, may give rise to an action for negligence.

Certificate of incorporation: A certificate issued by CRO on the registration of a company. The certificate is conclusive evidence that the company has been registered and that all the statutory requirements in respect of registration have been complied with.

Civil law: Law governing disputes between private individuals.

Glossary of Terms

Civil law system: System of law developed from the Roman Empire and used in parts of Europe (France and Germany). A feature is codification of law and an inquisitorial system of trial.

Claimant: The person who complains or brings an action asking the court for relief in the case, also called a plaintiff

Codification: The replacement of common law rules by statute which embodies those rules.

Common law: The body of legal rules developed by the common law courts and now embodied in legal decisions.

Compulsory winding up: liquidation, initiated when a creditor petitions the court.

Conciliation: The process whereby a third person, called a conciliator, listens to the two parties to a dispute and makes suggestions in an attempt to reach agreement.

Condition: Term which is vital to a contract. Breach of a condition destroys the basis of the contract which is itself then breached.

Consideration: Consists either in some right, interest, profit or benefit accruing to one party contract, or some forbearance, detriment, loss or responsibility given, suffered or undertaken by the other. Broadly, what each part contributes to the contract.

Constitution (company): A document which sets out the rules for governing a company and includes the articles of association and member resolutions. The term 'constitution' has now replaced the term 'memorandum and articles of association' in Ltd.'s.

Constitution (state): A document which sets out the rules whereby laws may be made in the state.

Contra proferentem: Courts can interpret any ambiguity against the person who relies on exclusion in a contract.

Contract: An agreement which legally binds the parties.

Contract of service/employment: A contract of employment is 'a contract of service or apprenticeship, whether express or implied, and (if it is express) whether it is oral or in writing.

Glossary of Terms

Contributory: A person liable to contribute to the assets of a company in a winding up. This includes present and certain past members, personal representatives of deceased members and trustees of bankrupt members.

Convention: An international multilateral treaty (between three or more parties), named a convention due to its importance, subject matter and/or number of signatories.

Creditors' voluntary winding up: A form of liquidation where a company does not provide a declaration of solvency. If no such declaration is made, the liquidation proceeds as a creditors' voluntary winding up even if in the end the company pays its debts in full.

Criminal law: A crime is conduct prohibited by the law of the state and tried in the criminal court system. It is punishable by the State.

Custom: Unwritten law which formed the basis of common law.

Damages: The sum claimed or awarded in a civil action in compensation for the loss or injury suffered by the claimant.

Defendant: The person against whom a civil action is brought or who is prosecuted for a criminal offence.

Delegated legislation: Rules of law made by subordinate bodies to whom the power to do so has been given by statute (also referred to as **subordinate legislation**).

Derivative claim: A remedy available to a minority shareholder to redress a wrong done to the company. Such an action is brought where those who have committed the offence control the company. Any benefit obtained will accrue to the company since the claim is derived from and made on behalf of the company.

Director: A person who takes part in making decisions and managing a company's affairs.

Distributable profit: Accumulated realised profits less accumulated realised losses.

Dividend: A distribution of profits to members made in proportion to their shareholdings.

Glossary of Terms

Equity: A source of law consisting of those rules which emerged from the Court of Chancery.

Exclusion clause Contract clause purporting to exclude or restrict liability.

Executed consideration: A performed, or executed, act in return for a promise.

Executory consideration: A promise given for a promise, not a performed act.

Express term A term that is clearly agreed to by the parties to a contract to be a term of that contract. In examining a contract, the courts will look first at the terms expressly agreed by the parties.

Fiduciary duty: A duty imposed upon certain persons because of the position of trust and confidence in which they stand in relation to another. The duty is more onerous than generally arises under a contractual or tort relationship. It requires full disclosure of information held by the fiduciary, a strict duty to account for any profits received as a result of the relationship, and a duty to avoid conflict of interest.

Fixed charge; A charge attaching to a particular asset on creation. The asset in question is usually a fixed asset, which the company is likely to retain for a long period. If the company defaults in payment of the debt the holder can realise the asset to meet the debt. Fixed charges rank first in order of priority in a liquidation.

Floating charge: A charge on a class of assets of a company, present and future which changes in the ordinary course of the company's business. Until the holders enforce the charge the company may carry on business and deal with the assets charged. It attaches to the assets only on crystallisation.

Fraud: Using misrepresentation to obtain an unjust advantage in the knowledge that it is untrue, without belief in its truth or recklessly, not caring whether it be true or false.

Fraudulent trading: Carrying on business and incurring debts when there is to the knowledge of the directors no reasonable prospect that these debts will be repaid, i.e. with intent to defraud the creditors. Persons so acting may be liable for the debts of the company as the court may decide.

Freedom of contract: Principle that parties may contract on the terms which they choose.

Glossary of Terms

Fundamental breach: Doctrine developed by the courts as a protection against unreasonable exemption clauses in contracts.

Good faith: Fair and open action without any attempt to deceive or take advantage of knowledge of which the other party is unaware.

Implied term: Term deemed to form part of a contract even though not expressly mentioned by the parties.

Indemnity: Security against or compensation for loss.

Indictable offences: Are serious offences that can be tried by a judge or jury.

Injunction: An equitable remedy in which the court orders the other party to a contract to observe negative restrictions.

Intention to create legal relations: Element necessary for an agreement to become a legally binding contract.

International law: The system of law which governs relationships between states. There are two types of international law – public and private. Public law regulates the interrelationship of sovereign states and their rights and duties with regard to one another. Private international law regulates between conflicts of national laws.

Insolvency: The inability to pay creditors in full after realising all the assets of a business.

Insolvency practitioner: Persons acting as a liquidator, administrative receiver, administrator or supervisor of a voluntary arrangement must be insolvency practitioners, authorised by the professional body to which they belong or the relevant government department.

Invitation to treat: Indication that someone is prepared to receive offers with a view to forming a binding contract. It is not an offer in itself.

Judgment: A sentence or order of the court.

Judicial review: Application to the High Court (or the highest court in the country if not called the High Court) for relief from a wrongful act.

Jurisdiction:: The area over which a court has authority, which can be geographical or subject-based.

Glossary of Terms

Laissez-faire: Non-interference by governments in negotiations between citizens.

Law Reports: The principal reports of decided cases.

Lifting the veil (of incorporation) : A company is normally to be treated as a separate legal person from its members. 'Lifting the veil' means that the company is identified with its members or directors or that a group of companies is to be treated as a single commercial entity. An example of this is to prevent fraud.

Limited liability: Limitation of the liability of members to contribute to the assets of a business in the event of a winding up.

Liquidated damages: A fixed sum agreed by parties to a contract, and payable in the event of a breach.

Liquidator A person who organises a company's liquidation or winding up. His task is to take control of the company's assets with a view to their realisation and the payment of all debts of the company and distribution of any surplus to members.

Listed: Quoted on a recognised stock exchange.

Managing director: One of the directors of the company appointed to carry out overall day-to-day management functions.

Mediation: A process of solving disputes where a third party, a mediator, listens to the parties in dispute and assists them in reaching agreement.

Member: Shareholder of a company.

Members' voluntary winding up: A form of liquidation where the directors have made a declaration of solvency and either the members have passed a resolution that the company be wound up, or the company has come to the end of a period fixed for its existence.

Memorandum of association: Together with the articles of association, this defines what the company is and how its affairs are to be conducted. It gives details of the company's name, objects, capital and registered office. Used in the DAC and PLC's.

Minutes: A written, indexed record of the business transacted and decisions taken at a meeting. Company and Corporations law requires minutes to be kept of all company meetings. Minutes of general meetings should be available for inspection by members.

Misrepresentation: False statement made with the object of inducing the other party to enter into a contract.

Mitigate: To lessen the effect of any action or omission to act by the injured party.

Negligence: This may refer to the way in which an act is carried out, that is carelessly, or to the tort which arises when a person breaches a legal duty of care that is owed to another, thereby causing loss to that other.

Novation: Transaction whereby a creditor agrees to release an existing debtor and substitute a new one in his or her place.

Obiter dicta: Statements made by a judge 'by the way'.

Objects: The aims and purposes of a company.

Offer A definite promise to be bound on specific terms.

Ordinary resolution: A resolution carried by a simple majority of votes cast. Where no other resolution is specified, 'resolution' means an ordinary resolution.

Ordinary share: A share which gives the holder the right to participate in the company's surplus profit and capital. The dividend is payable only when preference dividends, including arrears, have been paid.

Partnership: The relation which subsists between persons carrying on a business in common with a view of profit. Every partner is liable without limit for the debts of the partnership.

Past consideration: Something already done at the time that a contractual promise is made.

Penalty clause: In a contract providing for a specific sum to be payable in the event of a subsequent breach.

Perpetual succession: The Company continues to exist despite the death, insolvency, or insanity of any member or director, any change in membership or any transfer of shares.

Glossary of Terms

Plaintiff: The person who complains or brings an action asking the court for relief in Ireland.

Precedent: A previous court decision.

Pre-registration contract: A contract purported to be made by a company or its agent before the company has received its certificate of registration. An agent may be made personally liable on such a contract which will be unenforceable against the company.

Private company: A company which may not offer shares to the public, and which has not been registered as a public company. Termed a proprietary company in Irish law.

Privity of contract: The relation between two parties to a contract.

Promoter (formator) : Person who undertakes to form a company by making the appropriate business preparations.

Public company: A company registered as such under Companies Act 2014 The principal distinction between public and private/proprietary companies is that only the former may offer shares to the public.

Quantum meruit: 'As much as he has deserved'. May be awarded in cases of breach of contract to reflect the value of the work done.

Quasi partnership: A small, usually private company, where the relationship between the directors is essentially like that of a partnership. The courts have taken into account the existence of such quasi-partnerships when applying the law.

Quorum: Minimum number required to be present for a valid meeting to take place.

Re: In the matter of. Seen in some case names.

Registered office A business address to which all communication with a company must be sent.

Registration: Process by which a company comes into being, which involves the filing of documents with the relevant authority and the issuance of a certificate of registration.

Glossary of Terms

Remoteness of damage: Relationship between a wrongful act and the resulting damage which determines whether or not compensation may be recovered. Different principles apply in contract and in tort.

Representation: Induces the formation of a contract but does not become a term of the contract. The importance of the distinction is that different remedies are available depending on whether a term is broken or a representation turns out to be untrue.

Repudiation: Rejection or renunciation.

Rescission: An equitable remedy through which a contract is cancelled or rejected and the parties are restored to their pre-contracted position.

Rule of law: The concept that all peoples and institutions in a sovereign state are governed by and subject to the law.

Sale of goods: A contract whereby the seller transfers or agrees to transfer the property in goods for a money consideration called the price.

Secretary (company): An officer of a company appointed to carry out general administrative duties. Every public company must have a secretary and a sole director must not also be the secretary.

Separation of powers: The distribution of powers between the three arms of government: the legislature, the executive, and the judiciary.

Shadow director: A person in accordance with whose instructions other directors are accustomed to act. **Share** A member's stake in a company's share capital.

Specific performance: An equitable remedy in which the court orders the defendant to perform his side of a contract.

Standard form contract: A standard document prepared by many large organisations and setting out the terms on which they contract with their customers.

Standard of proof: The extent to which the court must be satisfied by the evidence presented.

Stare Decisis: To stand by a decision.

Statute Law: (legislation) made by a legislature or by some other body in the exercise of law-making powers delegated by the legislature.

Glossary of Terms

Subordinate legislation: Rules of law made by subordinate bodies to whom the power to do so has been given by statute (also referred to as **delegated legislation**).

Subsidiary company: A company under the control of another company, its holding company.

Summary offences: Are minor crimes, only triable summarily in lower level courts.

Treaty: A formal agreement between two or more sovereign states.

Ultra Vires: Beyond their powers. In company law, this term is used in connection with transactions which are outside the scope of the objects clause and therefore, in principle at least, unenforceable.

Unenforceable contract: Is a valid contract and property transferred under it cannot be recovered even from the other party to the contract if either party refuses to perform the contract, the other party cannot compel him to do so.

Unlimited liability: Members do not have limited liability and in the event of liquidation members are required to contribute as much as needed to repay the company's debt in full.

Void contract: Not a contract at all. The parties are not bound by it and if they transfer property under it they can sometimes recover their goods even from a third party.

Voidable contract: A contract which one party may avoid, that is, terminate at his option. Property transferred before avoidance is usually irrecoverable from a third party.

Warranty: Minor term in a contract. It does not go to the root of the contract, but is subsidiary to the main purpose of the contract. Breach of a warranty does not give rise to breach of the contract itself.

Winding up: This is an insolvency procedure that applies to companies, it is otherwise known as liquidation. This may take the form of a compulsory winding up, a members' voluntary winding up or a creditors' voluntary winding up.

Wrongful trading (Fraudulent): The term used where directors of an insolvent company knew or should have known that there was no reasonable prospect that the company could have avoided insolvency and did not take sufficient steps to minimise the potential loss to the creditors.

References

References

Accounting Technicians Ireland. (2013). Auditors Duties and Responsibilities - Chapter 13. In A. T. Ireland, ATI - Law and Ethics. ATI.

Advice, F. (2014). What is a contract. Retrieved April 2014, from Free Advice: http://law.freeadvice.com/general_practice/contract_law/contract_agreement.htm

All Business. (2011). Mortgage Definition. Retrieved 2014, from All Business Com: http://www.allbusiness.com/glossaries/mortgage/4944675-1.html

Ask about money. (2006). Deposits. Retrieved 2014, from Ask about money: http://www.askaboutmoney.com/showthread.php?t=34597

Askar. (2008, 11 5). Criminal case trial process. Retrieved April 2014, from ASk About Money: http://www.askaboutmoney.com/showthread.php?t=95905

BASIS. (2011). Consumer Rights. Retrieved May 2014, from Basis: http://www.basis.ie/home/home.jsp?pcategory=14537&ecategory=14540&doclistid=14542&sectionpage=&language=EN&page=&link=link001&doc=11710&logname=The%20Office%20of%20the%20Director%20of%20Consumer%20Affairs%5B1%5D&urlcode=

BASIS. (2014). EMPLOYEE RIGHTS. Retrieved 2014, from BASIS: http://www.basis.ie/home/home.jsp?pcategory=13887&ecategory=13913&sectionpage=10339&language=EN&page=&link=link001&doc=11333&doclistid=18018&logname=Contract%20of%20Employment%5B1%5D&urlcode=

BASIS. (2014). Leave Entitlements. Retrieved 2014, from BASIS: http://www.basis.ie/home/home.jsp?pcategory=12823&ecategory=12908&language=EN&link=link003&doc=11353&doclistid=18214&logname=Holiday%20Entitlements%5B1%5D

BASIS. (2014). Night Worker Regulations. Retrieved MAy 2014, from BASIS: http://www.basis.ie/home/home.jsp?pcategory=12823&ecategory=12917&doclistid=12919&sectionpage=10339&language=EN&page=&link=link003&doc=10770&logname=Night%20Worker%20Regulation&urlcode=

Basis.ie. (2009). Interim Orders. Retrieved 2014, from Basis : http://www.basis.ie/home/home.jsp?pcategory=13188&ecategory=13215&sectionpage=10339&language=GA&page=&link=link001&doc=10938&doclistid=13220&logname=Remedies%20%C2%96%20Interim%20Orders&urlcode=

Beauchamps. (2008). Commercial Property Update. Retrieved May 2014, from Beauchamps Solicitors: www.beauchamps.ie/downloads/CP%20update%20October%202010.pdf

Bills and Legislation. (2014). Retrieved April 2014, from Houses of the Oireachtas: http://www.oireachtas.ie/parliament/oireachtasbusiness/billslegislation/

Biz Types. (2014). Sole trader. Retrieved 2014, from Business Enterprise: http://www.businessenterprisedev.org/biz_types.html

Blurtit. (2014). What Are Negotiable Instrument? And Examples Of Negotiable Instrument. Retrieved 2014, from Business and Finance: http://business-finance.blurtit.com/1129915/what-are-negotiable-instrument-and-examples-of-negotiable-instrument

Boundless. (2012). Sole Proprietorships. Retrieved MAy 2014, from Boundless: https://www.boundless.com/business/types-of-business-ownership/sole-proprietorships/a-brief-definition-of-sole-proprietorships/

Bright Contracts. (2014). Employee contracts. Retrieved 2014, from Bright Contracts: http://www.brightcontracts.ie/docs/employees-and-contracts/employees/

Citizen Information. (2014). Unfair Dismissal - Employment. Retrieved 2014, from Citizen Information.

Citizen Information. (2014). Glossary of debt terms. Retrieved 2014, from Citizen Information: http://www.citizensinformation.ie/en/money_and_tax/personal_finance/debt/glossary_of_debt_terms.html

References

Citizens Information. (2010). Employment rights. Retrieved 2014, from Citizens Information: http://www.citizensinformationboard.ie/publications/providers/downloads/employment_rights_10.pdf

Citizens Information. (2014). Courts System. Retrieved April 2014, from Citizens Information : http://www.citizensinformation.ie/en/justice/courts_system/district_court.html

Citizens Information. (2014). Employment Working Time (Records). Retrieved May 2014, from Citizens Information: http://www.citizensinformation.ie/en/employment/employment_rights_and_conditions/hours_of_work/employment_working_time_records.html

Citizens Information. (2014). Supreme Court of Ireland. Retrieved May 2014, from Citizen Information: http://www.citizensinformation.ie/en/justice/courts_system/supreme_court.html

Citizens Information. (2014). Your consumer rights. Retrieved 2014, from Citizen Information: http://www.citizensinformation.ie/en/consumer_affairs/consumer_protection/consumer_rights/consumers_and_the_law_in_ireland.html

Cleary. (2011). Unfair Dismiss. Retrieved 2014, from Cleary & Co Solicitors: http://clearysolicitors.ie/employment-law/unfair-dismissal/

Consumer Association of Ireland. (2010). Legal Protection. Retrieved May 2014, from Consumer Protection Association: http://thecai.ie/your-rights/legal-protection/

Consumer Connect. (2009). Small Claims Court Ireland - get all your consumer information on Consumer Connect.ie. Retrieved 2014, from Consumer Connect: http://www.consumerconnect.ie/eng/Get_Your_Rights/Going_To_Court_Guide/

Contactlaw.ie. (2014). Breach of Contract. Retrieved April 2014, from Contact Law: http://www.contactlaw.ie/five-faqs-on-breach-of-contract.html

Citizens Information (2010) [online], available from http://www.citizensinformation.ie/en/ [accessed 2 June 2011].

Clyne, T (2014) Business law in Ireland, Oiliuna, Dublin

Clyne, T (2015) An Introduction to the Irish Legal System; Retrieved 2014; http://teresaclyne.com/

Contract Law; 2007; Paul A. McDermott (Butterworths) as referenced @. Mason Hayes and Curran. [ONLINE] Available at: http://www.google.ie/url?sa=t&rct=j&q=&esrc=s&source=web&cd=6&cad=rja&uact=8&ved=0ahUKEwjZgfTstdbKAhUCdw8KHYadDHQQFghHMAU&url=http%3A%2F%2Fwww.mhc.ie%2Fuploads%2FChange_in_privity_of_contract_rules_230107.pdf&usg=AFQjCNFMc5Z32OO997PIQE5XonkobTTSUQ&sig2=2BMsBXO5FD2usejmak9Y6Q&bvm=bv.113034660,d.ZWU. [Accessed 03 February 16].

Contract e-book. 2013. Contract e-book. [ONLINE] Available at: http://legalmax.info/conbook/index.htm#t=atlas_ex.htm. [Accessed 10 May 15].

Citizens Information (2010) [online], available from http://www.citizensinformation.ie/en/ [accessed 2 June 2011].

Contract Law; 2007; Paul A. McDermott (Butterworths) as referenced @. Mason Hayes and Curran. [ONLINE] Available at: http://www.google.ie/url?sa=t&rct=j&q=&esrc=s&source=web&cd=6&cad=rja&uact=8&ved=0ahUKEwjZgfTstdbKAhUCdw8KHYadDHQQFghHMAU&url=http%3A%2F%2Fwww.mhc.ie%2Fuploads%2FChange_in_privity_of_contract_rules_230107.pdf&usg=AFQjCNFMc5Z32OO997PIQE5XonkobTTSUQ&sig2=2BMsBXO5FD2usejmak9Y6Q&bvm=bv.113034660,d.ZWU. [Accessed 03 February 16].

Courts Service. (2006). District Court. Retrieved April 2014, from Courts Service: http://www.courts.ie/courts.ie/library3.nsf/pagecurrent/E110997F0240362D80256D8700505112?opendocument&l=en

References

Courts Service. (2009). History of the state. Retrieved from Courts Service: http://www.courts.ie/Courts.ie/library3.nsf/pagecurrent/8B9125171CFBA78080256DE5004011F8?opendocument

Courts Service. (2014). History of the Law. Retrieved 2014, from Courts service: http://www.courts.ie/Courts.ie/library3.nsf/pagecurrent/8B9125171CFBA78080256DE5004011F8?opendocument

CPA Ireland. (2011). Corporate Governance. Retrieved 2014, from CPA IReland: Likewise of importance is that fact that employers are only vicariously liable for torts committed by employees who are under a contract of service. Independent contractors under a contract for services are responsible for their own torts.

Debt Questions. (2011). Debt Questions. Retrieved 2014, from Debt Questions: http://www.debtquestions.co.uk/debt_forum/viewtopic.php?f=7&t=23845&start=15

Department of Jobs Trade and Innovation. (2014). Consumer Policy Section: Primary legislation and associated secondary legislation. Retrieved 2014, from Department of Jobs Trade and Innovation: http://www.djei.ie/commerce/consumer/domesticlegislation.htm

Department of Enterprise, Trade and Employment. (2014). Organisation of Working Time. Retrieved 2014, from Department of Enterprise, Trade and Employment: http://www.cwu.ie/_uploads/documents/Labour_Law_Pdf/Organisation_and_Working_Time_Act_-_Explanatory_Guide.pdf

Doherty, C. a. (2010). Employment Law. Retrieved 2014, from CN Doherty: http://www.cndoherty.ie/index.cfm/practice-areas/employment/

E2-P. (2014). Consumer Rights. Retrieved 2014, from E2-P: http://www.e2-p.eu/en-ie/keyquestions/what-rights-do-customers-have

Employment Rights Ireland. (2010). Employment law. Retrieved 2014, from Employment Rights Ireland: http://employmentrightsireland.com/unfair-dismissals-and-constructive-dismissal-in-ireland-the-facts-you-should-know/

Elaw Cases. 2010. ElawResources. [ONLINE] Available at: http://e-lawresources.co.uk/cases/Schawel-v-Reade.php. [Accessed 01 November 15].

E-law Resources. 2013. Contract Law Duress. [ONLINE] Available at: http://www.e-lawresources.co.uk/North-Ocean-Shipping-v-Hyundai-Construction-%28The-Atlantic-Baron%29.php. [Accessed 01 February 16].

FLAC. (2012). Working Time. Retrieved 2014, from Free Legal Advice Centre: www.flac.ie/download/pdf/working_hours_09.pdf

Flynn and O'Driscoll. (2010). Annual Returns. Retrieved 2014, from Flynn & O'Driscoll: http://www.fod.ie/Doing_Business_in_Ireland_Compliance_Requirements_of_an_Irish_Registered_Company_2013.pdf

FormaCompany. (2009). Company Secretary. Retrieved 2014, from FormaCompany: http://www.formacompany.com/en/ireland/company-formations/company-secretary

Formacompany. (2011). Benefits of a Limited Company - Limited Liability - what does it really mean? Retrieved 2014, from FormaCompany: http://www.formacompany.ie/en/company-formations/benefits-of-a-limited-company

Gavin O'Flaherty, M. B. (2009). Partnerships . Retrieved 2014, from Mason, Hayes & Curran: http://www.mhc.ie/uploads/Irish_Tax_Review_Gavin_OFlaherty_Muireann_Brick_April_09.pdf

Geraghty Solicitors. (2011). Consumer Rights. Retrieved May 2014, from Geraghty Solicitors: http://www.solicitorsgalway.ie/consumer-law/consumer-rights/

Glynn, J. (2012). Redundancy. Retrieved May 2014, from John Glynn Solicitors: http://www.solicitor.net/employment-law/redundancy.214.html

Glynn, J. (2014). Directors Powers and Obligations. Retrieved 2014, from Hohn Glynn Solicitors: http://www.solicitor.net/company-commercial/powers-obligations.126.html

References

Group, F. S. (2009, March). Company law - Consequences of Incorporation. Retrieved May 2014, from FE1 Study Group: https://www.mail-archive.com/fe-1-study-group@googlegroups.com/msg01385.html

Hamcot. (2009). Leasing. Retrieved 2014, from Hamcot: http://www.hamcot.com/Leasing.html

Healy & O'Connor. (2014). Unfair Dismissals. Retrieved 2014, from Healy and O Connor: http://www.hoc.ie/private-law/employment-law/unfair-dismissals/

Hedley, Steve. 2012. Contract / Mistake. [ONLINE] Available at: http://www.stevehedley.com. [Accessed 17 July 15].

Hedley, Steve. 2012. Contract / Pressure [ONLINE] Available at: http://www.stevehedley.com. [Accessed 17 July 15].

Holmes O'Malley Sexton, Bishopsgate, Henry Street, Limerick, Ireland,. 2013. High Court Ruling on Undue Influence (15.11.2013). [ONLINE] Available at: http://www.homs.ie/whatsnew-publication-367-High_Court_Ruling_on_Undue_Influence_(15.11.2013). [Accessed 11 November 14].

High Court Ruling on Undue Influence (15.11.2013). [ONLINE] Available at: http://www.homs.ie/whatsnew-publication-367-High_Court_Ruling_on_Undue_Influence_(15.11.2013). [Accessed 11 November 14].

Hong Kong Land Law Blog. 2013. Barclays Bank plc v O'Brien: the risk of failing to take steps to ensure informed consent. [ONLINE] Available at: https://hklandlaw.wordpress.com/2013/10/01/barclays-bank-plc-v-obrien-the-risk-of-failing-to-take-steps-to-ensure-informed-consent/. [Accessed 11 November 14].

IRISH LAW: A STUDENT'S GUIDE (2012) IRISH LEGAL SYSTEM [accessed 2 June 2011]. https://lawinireland.wordpress.com/irish-legal-system/

Ireland, P. (2012, july). Vicarious Liability. Retrieved January 2, 2015, from Peninsula Ireland: https://thepeninsulairelandblog.wordpress.com/2012/07/25/vicarious-liability-implications-for-employers/

IRISH LAW: A STUDENT'S GUIDE (2012) CONTRACT LAW [accessed 2 June 2011]. https://lawinireland.wordpress.com/the-law-of-contract/

IRISH LAW: A STUDENT'S GUIDE (2012) CONTRACT LAW [accessed 2 June 2011]. https://lawinireland.wordpress.com/employment-law/

Information Ireland. (2009). Common law. Retrieved April 2014, from Information Ireland: http://www.ireland-information.com/reference/legalsys.html

Information Ireland. (2012, October). The Irish State - Legal System. Retrieved from http://www.ireland-information.com/reference/legalsys.html.

Information. C. (2014). High Court. Retrieved 2014, from Citizen Information: http://www.citizensinformation.ie/en/justice/courts_system/high_court.html

Inquisition. (2011). Common Law. Retrieved April 2014, from In Inquisition: http://theinquisition.eu/wordpress/2011/history/common-law/

Irish Constitution. (2009). Constitution of the Irish Free State. Retrieved April 2014, from Constitution of the Irish Free State: http://en.wikipedia.org/wiki/Constitution_of_the_Irish_Free_State

ISSUU. (2011). Know your rights. Retrieved May 2014, from Connemara View: http://issuu.com/connemaraview/docs/03_cv_apr08

Jackson, J. (2014). The understanding of the distinction between a contract for services and a contract of. Retrieved May 2014, from CPA Ireland: http://www.cpaireland.ie/docs/default-source/Students/Study-Support/P1-Corporate-Laws-Governance/contract-for-services-v-contract-of-services.pdf?sfvrsn=0

Jim Finn, B. (2009). Incorporation – the benefits. Retrieved 2014, from CPA IRELAND: http://www.cpaireland.ie/docs/default-source/Students/Study-Support/F1-Business-Laws/incorporation.pdf?sfvrsn=0

Keenan, A. (2008) Essentials of Irish Business Law, Fifth Edition, Dublin, Gill and Macmillan.

Lawteacher.Net. 2013. Exclusion Clauses Cases. [ONLINE] Available at: http://www.lawteacher.net/cases/contract-law/exclusion-clauses-cases.php. [Accessed 22 September 15].

Legal humour: 2015, [accessed 2 June 2017] https://www.pinterest.com/Alaska0567/legal-humor/

References

Liquidators, Receivers & Examiners under the Companies Act. Office of the Director of Corporate Enforcement. http://www.odce.ie/Portals/0/Liquidators,%20Receivers%20and%20Examiners.pdf

McCarthy, B. (2008). News. Dublin: http://votebrianmccarthy.com/category/news/.

Mondaq. (2009*2014). Ireland: Bulletin - Consumer Credit Act, 1995 In Force. Retrieved 2014, from Mondaq:http://www.mondaq.com/x/5156/Antitrust+Competition/Bulletin+Consumer+Credit+Act+1995+In+Force

National Consumer Agency. (2010). Car finance/Hire purchase. Retrieved 2014, from National Consumer Agency: http://www.consumerhelp.ie/car-finance

Newton, A. (2010). Employment Issues. Retrieved 2014, from IBEC: http://www.ibec.ie/IBEC/Publications.nsf/vPages/Corporate_Restructuring_Guidelines~employment-issues/$file/Employment%20Issues.pdf

NUI Galway. (2011). ANNUAL LEAVE AND PUBLIC HOLIDAY ENTITLEMENTS. Retrieved 2014, from NUI GALWAY: http://www.nuigalway.ie/hr/documents/annual_leave_policy__part_time_staff__march_2011.pdf

Mason Hayes and Curran. 2012. Taking security: the problem of "vulnerable" guarantors. [ONLINE] Available at: http://www.mhc.ie/latest/e-zines/litigation-risk-update-august-2012/P1. [Accessed 01 February 16].

Networked Knowledge. 2013. Networked Knowledge - Contract Law Casenotes. [ONLINE] Available at: http://netk.net.au/Contract/NorthOcean.asp. [Accessed 21 March 15].

Networked Knowledge. 2013. Contract Law Casenotes. [ONLINE] Available at: http://netk.net.au/Contract/Lewis.asp. [Accessed 01 February 16].

OmniPro. (2009). Liquidation. Retrieved 2014, from OmniPro: http://omniproaccountantsblog.blogspot.ie/

Overview of Irish Corporate Law. (2014). Retrieved 2014, from Irish Corporate Law Forum: http://iclf.ie/irish-corporate-law.php

Phelan, F. (2014). Employment law. Retrieved 2014, from F,G Phelan & Co Solicitors: http://fgphelan.ie/employment_law.php

Routledge. (2009). Contract Law. Retrieved 2014, from Routledge: http://www.routledge.com/cw/revision2/p/contract/

RTE. (2011). Know your rights. Retrieved 2014, from RTE: http://www.rte.ie/tv/valueformoney/rights4.html

Ryan, F. (2006). Contract Law. Dublin: Round Hall Nutshells, (Thomson Round Hall 2006).

Routledge. (2009). Contract Law. Retrieved 2014, from Routledge: http://www.routledge.com/cw/revision2/p/contract/

RTE. (2011). Know your rights. Retrieved 2014, from RTE: http://www.rte.ie/tv/valueformoney/rights4.html

Ryan, F. (2006). Contract Law, . Dublin: Round Hall Nutshells, (Thomson Round Hall 2006).

Separate legal personality,. (2001, Jan). Retrieved 2014, from separate legal personality,: http://www.multitran.ru/c/m.exe?a=4&MessNum=179356&l1=1&l2=2

Sixth Form Law. (2006). Sixth form law. Retrieved April 2014, from What is law: http://sixthformlaw.info/01_modules/other_material/law_and_morality/0_what_is_law.htm

Solicitor, M. (2014). Employment law. Retrieved 2014, from My Solicitor.net: http://www.my-solicitor.net/index.php/employment-law/unfair-dismissal

Solicitors in Ireland. (2012). Consumer Law in Ireland. Retrieved May 2014, from Solicitors in Ireland: http://www solicitorsinireland.com/Consumer_Law%20_Solicitor_Ireland.html

StudyMode. (2011). Company Law. Retrieved 2014, from StudyMode: http://www.studymode.com/essays/Company-Law-696791.html

StudyMode. (2011). From My Heart to the Heavens. Retrieved 2014, from Study Mode: http://www.studymode.com/essays/From-My-Heart-To-The-Heavens-1219710.html

Sale of Goods and Supply of Services Act, 1980. 2010. Irish Statute Book. [ONLINE] Available at: http://www.irishstatutebook.ie/eli/1980/act/16/enacted/en/html. [Accessed 02 September 14].

References

Sixth Form Law. (2006). Sixth form law. Retrieved April 2014, from; What is law: http://sixthformlaw.info/01_modules/other_material/law_and_morality/0_what_is_law.htm

Stare Decisis law reports- Ciaran Joyce BL. 2012. Correct test not applied in assessing whether defendant had actual knowledge of alleged misrepresentation. [ONLINE] Available at: http://www.staredecisishibernia.com/correct-test-not-applied-assessing-whether-defendant-actual-knowledge-alleged-misrepresentation/. [Accessed 01 February 16].

Swarb.co.uk. 2015. Unconscionable contract. [ONLINE] Available at: http://swarb.co.uk/boustany-v-piggott-pc-1995/. [Accessed 01 February 16].

Taxman, J. (2013, July). Product returns. Retrieved 2014, from Backroads Forum: http://www.backroads.ie/forums/archive/index.php/t-11034.html

Temba, F. M. (2013). The evolution and the changing face in contract. Retrieved 2014, from Open University: file:///C:/Users/others/Downloads/33-94-1-PB.pdf

Tompkin (2014) [ONLINE] Last accessed 2 July 2012 www.jsijournal.ie/.../4%5B2%5D_Tomkin

The Brehon Laws. (2011). Retrieved April 2014, from Brehon Law: http://brehonlaw-justice.blogspot.ie/2013/03/the-brehon-law.html

Unemployment in Ireland. (2010). Redundancy Information. Retrieved May 2014, from unemployment in Ireland: http://www.unemploymentireland.com/redun.html

Union Connect. (2010). Directors Responsibilities. Retrieved 2014, from Union Connect: www.unionconnect.ie

What is a Statutory Instrument. (2012). Retrieved 2014 April, from Stephen Donnelly: http://stephendonnelly.ie/what-is-a-statutory-instrument/

Wikipedia. (2011). Law of the Republic of Ireland. Retrieved April 2014, from Wikipedia: http://en.wikipedia.org/wiki/Law_of_the_Republic_of_Ireland

Wikia Case Briefs. 2010. Case Law Thornton v Shoe Lane Parking Ltd.. [ONLINE] Available at: http://casebrief.wikia.com/wiki/Thornton_v_Shoe_Lane_Parking_Ltd.. [Accessed 02 September 14].

Wikipedia. 2012. Barton v Armstrong. [ONLINE] Available at: https://en.wikipedia.org/wiki/Barton_v_Armstrong. [Accessed 08 October 15].

Wikipedia. 2011. Edgington v Fitzmaurice - Misrepresentation. [ONLINE] Available at: https://en.wikipedia.org/wiki/Edgington_v_Fitzmaurice. [Accessed 01 February 16].

Woods, Kieron (2011) The Irish Legal System [ONLINE] Last accessed 2 July 2012 http://irishbarrister.com/legalterms.html

Work Place Relations. (2009). Guide to labour law. Retrieved 2014, from Work Place Relations: www.workplacerelations.ie/en/Publications.../Guide_to_Labour_Law.pdf

Yangysnu. (2006). Irish State. Retrieved April 2014, from zhidao: http://zhidao.baidu.com/question/1384507.html

CPSIA information can be obtained
at www.ICGtesting.com
Printed in the USA
LVHW101339190921
698210LV00009B/377

9 781530 010226